Great Careers

Construction and Trades

with a High School Diploma

D0068777

Titles in the *Great Careers* series

Great Careers

Construction and Trades

with a High School Diploma

Kenneth C. Mondschein

Ferguson Publishing
An imprint of Infobase Publishing

Great Careers with a High School Diploma
Construction and Trades

Ferguson
An imprint of Infobase Publishing
132 West 31st Street
New York, NY 10001

ISBN-13:978-0-8160-7043-5

Library of Congress Cataloging-in-Publication Data

Great careers with a high school diploma. — 1st ed.
     v. cm.
  Includes bibliographical references and index
  Contents: [1] Food, agriculture, and natural resources — [2] Construction and trades — [3] Communications, the arts, and computers — [4] Sales, marketing, business, and finance — [5] Personal care services, fitness, and education — [6] Health care, medicine, and science — [7] Hospitality, human services, and tourism — [8] Public safety, law, and security — [9] Manufacturing and transportation — [10] Armed forces.
  ISBN-13: 978-0-8160-7046-6 (v.1)
  ISBN-10: 0-8160-7046-6 (v.1)
  ISBN-13: 978-0-8160-7043-5 (v.2)
  ISBN-10: 0-8160-7043-1 (v.2)
[etc.]
1. Vocational guidence — United Sates. 2. Occupations — United Sates. 3. High school graduates — Employment — United Sates.
  HF5382.5.U5G677 2007
  331.702'330973 — dc22

                                                                    2007029883

Ferguson books are available at special discounts when purchased in bulk quantities for businesses, associations, institutions, or sales promotions. Please call our Special Sales Department in New York at (212) 967-8800 or (800) 322-8755.

You can find Ferguson on the World Wide Web at
http://www.fergpubco.com

Produced by Print Matters, Inc.
Text design by A Good Thing, Inc.
Cover design by Salvatore Luongo

Printed in the United States of America

Sheridan PMI 10 9 8 7 6 5 4 3 2 1

This book is printed on acid-free paper.

Contents

How to Use This Book

This book, part of the Great Careers with a High School Diploma series, highlights in-demand careers that require no more than a high school diploma or the general educational development (GED) credential and offers opportunities for personal growth and professional advancement to motivated readers who are looking for a field that's right for them. The focus throughout is on the fastest-growing jobs with the best potential for advancement in the field. Readers learn about future prospects while discovering jobs they may never have heard of.

Knowledge—of yourself and about a potential career—is a powerful tool in launching yourself professionally. This book tells you how to use it to your advantage, explore job opportunities, and identify a good fit for yourself in the working world.

Each chapter provides the essential information needed to find not just a job but a career that draws on your particular skills and interests. All chapters include the following features:

- ✶ "Is This Job for You?" presents a set of questions for you to answer about yourself to help you learn if you have what it takes to work in a given career.
- ✶ "Let's Talk Money" and "Lets Talk Trends" provide at a glance crucial information about salary ranges and employment prospects.
- ✶ "What You'll Do" provides descriptions of the essentials of each job.
- ✶ "Where You'll Work" relates the details of the settings and the rules and patterns typical of that field.
- ✶ "Your Typical Day" provides details about what a day on the job involves for each occupation.
- ✶ "The Inside Scoop" presents firsthand information from someone working in the field.
- ✶ "What You Can Do Now" provides advice on getting prepared for your future career.
- ✶ "What Training You'll Need" discusses state requirements, certifications, and courses or other training you may need as you get started on your new career path.
- ✶ "How to Talk Like a Pro" defines a few key terms that give a feel for the occupation.

- ⭐ "How to Find a Job" gives the practical how-tos of landing a position.
- ⭐ "Secrets for Success" and "Reality Check" share inside information on getting ahead.
- ⭐ "Some Other Jobs to Think About" lists similar related careers to consider.
- ⭐ "How You Can Move Up" outlines how people in each occupation turn a job into a career, advancing in responsibility and earnings power.
- ⭐ "Web Sites to Surf" lists Web addresses of trade organizations and other resources providing more information about the career.

In addition to a handy comprehensive index, the back of the book features an appendix providing invaluable information on job hunting strategies and techniques. This section provides general tips on interviewing, constructing a strong résumé, and gathering professional references. Use this book to discover a career that seems right for you—the tools to get you where you want to be are at your fingertips.

Introduction

For millions of Americans, life after high school means stepping into the real world. Each year more than 900,000 of the nation's 2.8 million high school graduates go directly into the workforce. Clearly, college isn't for everyone. Many people learn best by using their hands rather than by sitting in a classroom. Others find that the escalating cost of college puts it beyond reach, at least for the time being. During the 2005–2006 school year, for instance, tuition and fees at a four-year public college averaged $5,491, not including housing costs, according to The College Board.

The good news is that there's a wide range of exciting, satisfying careers available without a four-year bachelor's degree or even a two-year associate's degree. Great Careers with a High School Diploma highlights specific, in-demand careers in which individuals who have only a high school diploma or the general educational development (GED) credential can find work, with or without further training (outside of college). These jobs span the range from apprentice electronics technician to chef, teacher's assistant, Webpage designer, sales associate, and lab technician. The additional training that some of these positions require may be completed either on the job, through a certificate program, or during an apprenticeship that combines entry-level work and class time.

Happily, there's plenty of growth in the number of jobs that don't require a college diploma. That growth is fastest for positions that call for additional technical training or a certificate of proficiency. The chief economist at the Economic Policy Foundation, a think tank, notes that there are simply more of these positions available than there are workers to fill them. In fact, only 23 percent of the jobs available in the coming years will require a four-year degree or higher, the foundation reports.

It's often said that higher education is linked to higher earnings. But this is not the whole story. Correctional officer, computer network technician, and electrician are just a few of the careers that offer strong income-earning potential. What's more, the gap that exists between the wages of high school graduates and those with college degrees has begun to close slightly. Between 2000 and 2004, the yearly earnings of college graduates dropped by 5.6 percent while the earnings of high school graduates increased modestly by 1.6 percent according to the Economic Policy Foundation. High school graduates earn a median yearly income of $26,104, according the U.S. Census Bureau.

So what career should a high school graduate consider? The range is so broad that Great Careers with a High School Diploma includes 10 volumes, each based on related career fields from the Department of Labor's career clusters. Within each volume approximately 10 careers are profiled, encouraging readers to focus on a wide selection of job possibilities, some of which readers may not even know exist. To enable readers to narrow their choices, each chapter offers a self-assessment quiz that helps answer the question, "Is this career for me?" What's more, each job profile includes an insightful look at what the position involves, highlights of a typical day, insight into the work environment, and an interview with someone on the job.

An essential part of the decision to enter a particular field includes how much additional training is needed. Great Careers features opportunities that require no further academic study or training beyond high school as well as those that do. Readers in high school can start prepping for careers immediately through volunteer work, internships, academic classes, technical programs, or career academies. (Currently, for instance, one in four students concentrates on a vocational or technical program.) For each profile, the best ways for high school students to prepare are featured in a "What You Can Do Now" section.

For readers who are called to serve in the armed forces, this decision also provides an opportunity to step into a range of careers. Every branch of the armed forces from the army to the coast guard offers training in areas including administrative, construction, electronics, health care, and protective services. One volume of Great Careers with a High School Diploma is devoted to careers than can be reached with military training. These range from personnel specialist to aircraft mechanic.

Beyond military options, other entry-level careers provide job seekers with an opportunity to test-drive a career without a huge commitment. Compare the ease of switching from being a bank teller to a sales representative, for instance, with that of investing three years and tens of thousands of dollars into a law school education, only to discover a dislike for the profession. Great Careers offers not only a look at related careers, but also ways to advance in the field. Another section, "How to Find a Job," provides job-hunting tips specific to each career. This includes, for instance, advice for teacher assistants to develop a portfolio of their work. As it turns out, employers of entry-level workers aren't looking for degrees and academic achievements. They want employability skills: a sense of responsibility, a willingness to learn, discipline, flexibility, and above all, enthusiasm. Luckily, with 100 jobs profiled in Great Careers with a High School Diploma, finding the perfect one to get enthusiastic about is easier than ever.

Work with your hands

Carpenter or Carpentry Assembler and Repairer

See your finished work take shape before your eyes

Help build everything from birdhouses to skyscrapers

Carpenter or Carpentry Assembler and Repairer

Carpentry likely was invented by the first person who discovered that tree branches could be joined together to make a shelter from the rain. Ever since then, carpenters have played an important part in society. In the Middle Ages, they were among the best-paid of skilled laborers. Their patron saint was St. Joseph, who, we are told, was himself a carpenter. Today, carpenters build everything from kitchen cabinets to entire houses. They are among the most skilled of laborers, and their work is always in high demand. There are about 1.3 million carpenters working in the United States today.

Is This Job for You?

To find out if being a carpenter is right for you, read each of the following questions and answer "Yes" or "No."

Yes   No   **1.** Do you like working with your hands?

Yes   No   **2.** Can you follow instructions?

Yes   No   **3.** Are you good at math and geometry?

Yes   No   **4.** Are you a precise worker?

Yes   No   **5.** Do you like planning your work out before doing it?

Yes   No   **6.** Do you work well with others?

Yes   No   **7.** Do people consider you patient?

Yes   No   **8.** Are you in good physical condition?

Yes   No   **9.** Can you communicate well in both Spanish and English?

Yes   No   **10.** Are you careful, especially with tools?

If you answered "Yes" to most of these questions, you might want to consider a career as a carpenter. To find out more about this job, read on.

What You'll Do

When you think of carpentry, the first thing you think of is wood. Carpenters use many materials, though, including drywall, fiberglass, and plastic. Carpenters work on everything from huge public works projects to small home-refinishing projects. A good carpenter can build an entire

Let's Talk Money

The median income for carpenters is $16.78 per hour, ranging from $10.36 to $28.65, according to 2006 data from the Bureau of Labor Statistics. More experienced carpenters, as well as those who work for contractors who make nonresidential buildings, tend to make the most. Less experienced carpenters and those who work for employment services tend to make the least. Because the availability of carpentry work varies with the weather and the construction market, carpenters' earnings are very dependent on both the weather and the economy.

house by him- or herself—framing and installing walls, floors, and doors, putting in the windows, building stairs, installing kitchen cabinets and the other furniture, and finishing up by hanging a birdhouse outside! Carpentry skills are also needed for things you wouldn't expect carpenters to work on, such as braces for tunnels, scaffolding, forms for concrete, and anything else needed for construction.

Of all the tools in a carpenter's toolbox, the most important is probably a ruler. "Measure twice, cut once" is the carpenter's motto. All carpentry projects begin with measuring and laying out the work, paying careful attention to the plans. Only then does the carpenter begin cutting the materials and shaping them with power and hand tools such as saws, planers, and sanders. The materials are then put together with nails, screws, and glue. Finally, carpenters use levels, plumb lines, and framing squares to check their work. While prefabricated components may make the job easier, the essentials of carpentry have not changed in thousands of years.

Who You'll Work For

✯ Large office, commercial, and industrial construction firms
✯ Specialty contractors, such as home renovators

Let's Talk Trends

The number of carpenters will grow about as fast as the average for all professions through 2014, according to the U.S. Bureau of Labor Statistics. Skilled carpenters are often hard to find and so are in high demand from contractors. There is also a high rate of turnover, as less-skilled carpenters leave the profession or look for less strenuous work.

⭐ Private homeowners and business owners
⭐ Local, state, and national governments
⭐ Self-employment

Where You'll Work

Carpenters can be found on any building site or in any community in North America. They are hired by companies who build everything from industrial parks to Little League fields, as well as by specialty businesses such as interior decorators. Over one-third of carpenters are self-employed. Some have their own businesses, either as general contractors or as specialists who build one particular item such as staircases or ornamental furniture. A highly skilled carpenter can move easily from one sort of carpentry to another, depending on what is in demand.

A carpenter's hours can be very irregular. Bad weather can delay or cancel outdoor work. Because of this, carpenters' work tends to be seasonal. Carpenters get more work in the summer and less in the winter. Those who live in places where the weather is generally good year-round, such as the South and Southwest, can work more days out of the year.

Carpentering can also be very strenuous. Carpenters are required to stand, climb, bend, kneel, stretch, squeeze into tight spaces, and lift and carry heavy loads. Working with power tools can also be dangerous if you're not careful. Also, because much of the work is outdoors, you will be exposed to sun, rain, heat, and cold.

Your Typical Day

Here are the highlights of a typical day for a carpenter.

✓ **Get there early.** Today you've been hired to put in some new kitchen cabinets in a family home. You know it's going to be a big job, so you arrive early.
✓ **Out with the old.** Before putting in the new cabinets, you have to take out the old ones. After draping the kitchen with a dust-cover, you carefully disassemble the old cabinets—making sure not to damage the walls, as well as to keep the family's five-year-old son and golden retriever away from the work area!
✓ **Measure twice.** The new cabinets are prefabricated, but they still

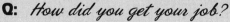

The Inside Scoop: Q&A

William J. Omar
Carpenter
Hull, Massachusetts

Q: *How did you get your job?*

A: I work for myself and for a real-estate company doing renovations and repairs. For the real-estate company, I answered an ad in our local newspaper, the *Patriot-Ledger*.

Q: *What do you like best about your job?*

A: Since I'm self-employed, I like to be able to work by myself and choose my own hours.

Q: *What's the most challenging part of your job?*

A: The real world isn't cut at 90-degree angles, and materials are often imperfect. The most challenging part of my job is making things come together that do not have perfect surfaces or angles.

Q: *What are the keys to success as a carpenter?*

A: Patience. Don't rush. The most important thing is being able to take your time with a project and have the end result turn out great!

have to be assembled carefully. Later there won't be any way to fix a botched job. After double-checking the assembly, you carefully put the new cabinets in place.

What You Can Do Now

✸ Know your way around a toolbox. Small projects at home or in shop class can familiarize you with how to work with wood and other materials.

✸ Pay attention in school. Carpenters need to be good at math and geometry. If you want to work as a contractor, it is also helpful to know Spanish because so many people in the trades are native speakers.

✳ If you are 18 or older, get a job as a carpenter's helper. You can begin learning on the job now.

What Training You'll Need

Carpenters can learn their work through formal training programs and apprenticeships, but many learn on the job by working as a carpenter's helper. Large construction companies with union membership sometimes offer apprenticeships. In these, on-the-job training is combined with classroom instruction, and you will be able to earn money while you learn. However, relatively few carpenters learn their trade this way, and such programs are also hard to get into.

Public or private trade schools are another way to learn carpentry. While you will have to pay money for your training, many of these schools are associated with large contractors or with unions that can help you find a job after you graduate. You will often find that employers look favorably on graduates of these schools, and you may also begin with a higher salary. Like apprenticeships, trade schools also give a combination of practical and classroom instruction.

Finally, you can find a carpenter and ask him or her to teach you the trade in return for your assistance as a carpenter's helper. This is perhaps the oldest form of apprenticeship—trading labor for knowledge.

In any program, you will learn the elements of carpentry—how to draw and read plans, elementary structure design, how to lay out work, how to use your tools, and how to do basic carpentry jobs. Generally, it takes three to four years of training to become a skilled carpenter. Essential academic skills are math, algebra, and geometry. English and Spanish classes will help you with your communications skills. It also helps to have good hand-eye coordination, a good level of physical fitness, and a good sense of balance. Carpenters should also be patient and detail-oriented: It takes only one mistake to ruin a whole afternoon's work.

How to Talk Like a Pro

Here are a few words you'll hear as a carpenter:

✳ **Level** Levels are used to find if a surface is horizontal. Originally a tube of water with a bubble in it that would float to the high end, many today are electronic.

☆ **Contractor** A contractor is hired to do a specific job, from small tasks such as refinishing a room to big ones such as public works projects. For complex tasks, a contractor may hire *subcontractors*.

☆ **Miter box** Carpenters have to cut wood or other materials at different angles. A miter box has grooves cut into it at known angles. By putting your material in the box and cutting in the grooves, you can be sure that the pieces will line up in the end.

How to Find a Job

Since skilled carpenters are always in demand, they have many ways of finding jobs. If you complete an apprenticeship through a contractor or union, you are almost guaranteed a job. Most unions also maintain a job board and help their members find work. Job placement is one of the many services unions provide, of course. They also can provide medical insurance and help pay unemployment when you're between jobs.

Other carpenters find jobs through advertisements placed by government agencies, manufacturing firms, or retail businesses that need a carpenter on-staff. Carpenters, especially the self-employed, can also find work through newspaper ads, word of mouth, or advertising themselves in the local newspaper or the Internet. Some Web sites, such as Craigslist (http://www.craigslist.org), that are good places to hire carpenters are also good spots to let the world know you're available to work.

No matter what, always make sure to put your best foot forward: If you do a good job, companies you have worked for in the past will be eager to hire you for more work.

Secrets for Success

See the suggestions below and turn to the appendix for advice on résumés and interviews.

☆ Learn Spanish. Since many people working in construction come from foreign countries, being able to make yourself understood in a second language can be very helpful.

☆ Be patient and painstaking. Wood is a very unforgiving material. Make one mistake, and the whole project can be ruined.

Reality Check

Carpentry can be both physically and mentally demanding. If you make a mistake, there may be no way to go back and fix it. It is also rather strenuous, and working with power tools can be dangerous. Many carpenters leave the profession every year for less demanding jobs.

Some Other Jobs to Think About

* Plumber or pipe fitter. Plumbers and pipe fitters are to the insides of walls what carpenters are to the surfaces. They connect buildings to the municipal water supply and make sure the plumbing works correctly.
* Electrician. Electricians are essential to modern construction, making sure the electrical system works properly.
* Concrete or brick mason. Rather than working in wood, concrete and brick masons work in materials that need less shaping, but no less precision.

How You Can Move Up

* Become a construction supervisor. Carpenters are more likely than any other tradespersons to become a foreman or supervisor. Here, knowledge of Spanish will really help communicate with your workers!
* Become an inspector. With their good all-around knowledge of building construction, carpenters are in a good position to become state or city safety inspectors.
* Go into business for yourself. About one third of carpenters are self-employed—more than any other construction trade.

Web Sites to Surf

United Brotherhood of Carpenters and Joiners of America (UBC). 520,000 members strong, the UBC provides a number of services to men and women working in construction trades. http://www.carpenters.org

Registered Apprenticeship Website. The U.S. Department of Labor's links to help you find apprenticeships in carpentry and other trades. http://www.doleta.gov/atels%5Fbat

Make a good wage

Construction Laborer or Construction-Equipment Operator

Build something of lasting value

Operate powerful machinery

Construction Laborer or Construction-Equipment Operator

In ancient Babylonia, a construction worker who did a bad job might be executed by the king. While our laws are no longer quite as strict, the construction industry has no less of a need for skilled laborers than it did in ancient times. Construction laborers are the men and women who build our nation's homes, schools, and office buildings. Without their work, our economy would grind to a halt. Empty fields and farmland wouldn't be turned into new housing developments. Useless old buildings would never be turned into profitable new ones. This job can also be an entry into more skilled, more highly paid trades such as masonry and carpentry. There are about 1 million construction laborers and 449,000 construction-equipment operators working in the United States today. More than 683,200 people work in construction in Canada. The profession is predominantly male.

Is This Job for You?

To find out if being a construction laborer or construction-equipment operator is right for you, read each of the following questions and answer "Yes" or "No."

Yes	No	**1.**	Are you in good physical shape?
Yes	No	**2.**	Are you careful?
Yes	No	**3.**	Do you work well as part of a team?
Yes	No	**4.**	Can you follow directions?
Yes	No	**5.**	Do you not mind working irregular hours?
Yes	No	**6.**	Do you not mind getting your hands dirty?
Yes	No	**7.**	Do you have good hand-eye coordination?
Yes	No	**8.**	Do you like working outdoors?
Yes	No	**9.**	Can you operate heavy equipment?
Yes	No	**10.**	Can you communicate in English and Spanish?

If you answered "Yes" to most of these questions, you might be cut out for a career as an construction laborer or construction-equipment operator. To find out more, read on.

Let's Talk Money

The median income for construction laborers is $12.10 per hour, ranging from $7.71 to $23.61, according to 2006 figures from the U.S. Bureau of Labor Statistics. The median income for construction-equipment operators is $17.00 per hour, but can vary between $10.98 and $29.34. Those construction laborers involved in highway, street, and bridge construction tend to make the most, and those who work for building contractors, the least. Construction-equipment operators involved in highway, street, and bridge construction likewise tend to make the most, and those who are employed by state and local governments, the least.

What You'll Do

Construction laborers are found everywhere from underground mineshafts to wide-open desert highways to suburban backyards to "high steel" hundreds of feet above city streets. If there's a job that needs doing, they're the ones who do it—lifting and carrying, riveting and welding, clearing rubble and putting up walls. Some of the jobs are very easy and can be learned in minutes, and some are very difficult and require years of training. Most jobs are relatively safe, but some, such as asbestos removal, can be hazardous. The more skilled the labor and the more dangerous the job, the more construction laborers tend to earn.

There are few young children who aren't fascinated with powerful construction equipment. Becoming a construction-equipment operator can be like a childhood dream come to life. You'll use the heavy machinery, such as pile drivers, backhoes, bulldozers, and steamrollers that knock down old buildings, tear up earth, pave roads, and do the other heavy work needed for construction. Construction-equipment operators also set up and position their equipment. However, operating construction equipment is very skilled labor and requires a lot of training.

Who You'll Work For

✴ Private building and demolition contractors
✴ City, state, and the federal government
✴ Residential, industrial, and commercial construction companies

Where You'll Work

Construction laborers and construction-equipment operators work everywhere that things are built—small towns and big cities, residential and business districts, in underground mines and on offshore oil rigs. Those who work on highways and other roadways tend to use specialized equipment such as asphalt paving machines, graders, and steamrollers to ensure that the roadway is flat. Their job is explained more in detail in the section on road-crew members.

Construction laborers and construction-equipment operators' work is seasonal. Because they work outdoors, bad weather can result in the loss of a day's wages. But if you like working outdoors—even in heat, cold, and rain—you'll enjoy construction work. All construction trades tend to get more work in the summer and less in the winter.

Construction labor can be very strenuous. However, if you like exerting yourself by lifting and carrying heavy loads, climbing, and working on your feet, this is the job for you! Construction equipment can be noisy and uncomfortable to use, power tools can be dangerous or lead to repetitive-stress injuries, and some of the substances you may come in contact with—like asbestos or hot asphalt—may be dangerous. However, workers who deal with such things are well-paid.

Your Typical Day

Here are the highlights of a typical day for a construction laborer renovating an apartment building.

- ✓ **Unload the truck.** First thing in the morning, a truck rolls up with the day's supply of lumber, drywall, and masonry for the workers to use. Before work starts, you'll need to unload the materials.
- ✓ **Rip it out.** Construction laborers don't just put things up—they also help rip them down. The decor in this building is just too old-fashioned for the sorts of tenants the landlord wants to attract. The claw-foot bathtub and pedestal sink will have to be thrown out. With a crowbar, you rip out the 19th-century bathroom tiling so that modern linoleum can be put in.

✓ **Lend a hand.** A construction laborer must be versatile. One minute you find yourself ripping old molding off the wall. The next you hold a piece of drywall in place while a coworker secures it to divide one apartment into two. When you're done, the old tenants won't even be able to recognize this place!

The Inside Scoop: Q&A

Bryan Murphy
Construction laborer
Bristol, Wisconsin

Q: *How did you get your job?*

A: I met my current employer through a previous employer. The president of my current company knew my previous boss and they recommended me to him and he then thought of me when he went to hire for my current position.

Q: *What do you like best about your job?*

A: Nothing is ever the same from day to day. While it's stressful and possibly aggravating, it is never boring. I love a challenge and my job is a lot like a 3-D jigsaw/art project. I enjoy being the person in my company who can provide correct information and answers.

Q: *What's the most challenging part of your job?*

A: Now that I'm a supervisor, I have to get an incredibly diverse group of subcontractors to work together to create a product. Learning their language (literally) is an important part of the relationship building that gets things done. Also, dealing with surprises that arise as work progresses.

Q: *What are the keys to success as a construction laborer?*

A: Hard work!

What You Can Do Now

- ✦ Pay attention in school, especially in English, Spanish, and shop classes.
- ✦ Stay fit. The better shape you're in, the more you'll like working in construction.
- ✦ Learn to drive. While construction equipment usually requires special permits, operating a car is a good way to start.

What Training You'll Need

Construction laborers and construction-equipment operators receive a wide variety of training, from informal on-the-job training to formal apprenticeships and trade schools. In general, the more complicated the work, the more likely you will need formal training.

Beginning construction laborers often start as helpers, learning from more experienced workers. They perform the most basic tasks, such as unloading materials, clearing work sites, and carrying loads. While working in this capacity, a construction laborer may also attend a trade or vocational school to learn specialized tasks such as welding, riveting, or hazardous materials removal (such as asbestos). Such things can sometimes be taught on the job, but employers tend to look more favorably on job applicants with formal training. Such training will include the physical skill itself, as well as safety, blueprint-reading, and other skills. Programs may last from two to four years. A very few employers, mainly those connected with unions, also offer apprenticeship programs. However, there tend to be very few spots in such programs.

Like construction laborers, construction-equipment operators may learn on the job or at specialized technical schools. Training in

Let's Talk Trends

The number of construction laborers will grow more slowly than the average for all workers through 2014, while the number of construction-equipment operators will increase about as fast as the average, according to the Bureau of Labor Statistics. The construction industry is expected to grow less rapidly than it has in the past, but jobs will open up thanks to high worker turnover.

hydraulics and electronics may be necessary as construction equipment grows more and more technologically advanced. Some contractors offer apprenticeship programs through the International Union of Operating Engineers or the Associated General Contractors of America. Such programs include three years, or 6,000 hours, of on-the-job training, with 144 hours of classroom instruction per year. There are also some technical schools teaching the use of construction equipment. However, unlike welding equipment, construction machinery is large and very expensive and difficult to teach in a classroom environment. Before applying to such a school, you should contact employers in your area to see what they think of its training, and also whether it allows you to use actual equipment in realistic situations.

How to Talk Like a Pro

Here are a few words you'll hear as a construction laborer or construction-equipment operator:

- ✶ **Asbestos** Asbestos is a naturally-occurring mineral. Because it is fireproof, it was once widely used in construction. However, it was discovered that asbestos' small particles, when breathed in, can cause cancer. There is now a large industry devoted to cleaning it out of buildings.
- ✶ **GPS** A Global Positioning System tells you exactly where in the world you are, based on signals from orbiting satellites. Today GPS technology is sometimes used to make grading and leveling operations more precise.
- ✶ **GMAW** Gas Metal Arc Welding is a welding technique in which a wire electrode and a shielding gas are fed through the welding gun. It is one of the most common welding techniques used today.

How to Find a Job

Many employers will hire unskilled or semiskilled workers through such means as newspaper help-wanted ads. Word of mouth is also important, if you know who or where to ask. If you ask local contractors and construction companies, some will even take walk-ins, though it is helpful to have a personal reference. You may be trained in the necessary skills on the job, or, more rarely, allowed to join an apprenticeship program.

For the best job opportunities, however, it is best to already be a skilled laborer. Trade and vocational schools are your best bet. Employers like to know that their employees know what they're doing. This is especially true for construction-equipment operators, who are trusted to use large, expensive, and sometimes dangerous machinery. Many trade and vocational schools also have job-placement programs for their graduates.

Other ways of finding work in construction are local joint labor-management apprenticeship committees, apprenticeship agencies, and state employment services. You can look for these organizations on the Web. If you already have some experience in construction, unions often operate job-placement services for their members. However, to join a union, you will need to be already employed in a field.

Secrets for Success

See the suggestions below and turn to the appendix for advice on résumés and interviews.

✯ Learn a trade. Skilled workers are always in more demand—and paid more—than unskilled.
✯ Work well as a team. No job can be done by one person alone.
✯ Be safety conscious. If you take care of your coworkers, they will take care of you.

Reality Check

Construction is hard, tiring, and occasionally dangerous work. However, it can pay very well and be very rewarding.

Some Other Jobs to Think About

✯ Stone, brick, or cement mason. Masons also work in construction, though their specialized skills help them earn much more money.
✯ Carpenters. Carpenters have their own skill set plus often go into business for themselves as general contractors.
✯ Truck driver. If you prefer working alone, truck driving is well-paid and involves much less heavy lifting.

How You Can Move Up

✦ Learn a skill. Skilled workers, such as welders, make a lot more money.

✦ Become a supervisor. Construction supervisors are in charge of other construction laborers' work. Because today many construction laborers' first language is Spanish, it helps to be able to communicate both in English and Spanish.

✦ Become a safety inspector. Experienced construction workers can sometimes find jobs with city and state governments as safety inspectors.

Web Sites to Surf

Laborers Learn. An education and training resource for construction laborers. Registration required. http://www.laborerslearn.org

International Union of Operating Engineers (IUOE). The IUOE is the union for construction-equipment operators. http://www.iuoe.org

Earn a good salary

Painter or Paperhanger

Make homes and offices beautiful

Work in a variety of places

Painter or *Paperhanger*

As long as people have built houses and other buildings, they have painted them to look cleaner and brighter. In Dendera in Egypt, you can see paint that is thousands of years old. In the Middle Ages houses were covered with whitewash and interior walls were often painted with bright colors and designs. Wallpaper was invented in 200 B.C. by the Chinese. It became popular during the Renaissance with people who were not rich enough to afford cloth tapestries. Modern wallpaper with repeating patterns was invented in France in the 17th century. Today painting houses and putting up wallpaper is still a big business. There are about 486,000 painters and paperhangers working in the United States today.

Is This Job for You?

To find out if being a painter or paperhanger is right for you, read each of the following questions and answer "Yes" or "No."

Yes   No   **1.** Are you a careful and precise worker?

Yes   No   **2.** Do you have a good eye for color?

Yes   No   **3.** Are you patient and plan your work carefully?

Yes   No   **4.** Can you follow directions?

Yes   No   **5.** Do you work well as part of a team?

Yes   No   **6.** Are you in good physical shape?

Yes   No   **7.** Do you like working with your hands?

Yes   No   **8.** Do you have good hand-eye coordination?

Yes   No   **9.** Do you not mind getting dirty?

Yes   No   **10.** Are you not afraid of hard work?

If you answered "Yes" to most of these questions, you might want to think about a career as a painter or paperhanger. To find out more about these jobs, read on.

What You'll Do

A painter or paperhanger's job is more than just slapping a coat of paint on. First you must choose what sort of paint is best: Interior or exterior? Smooth or glossy? Some paints are meant for use outdoors. An interior paint used on the outside of a building will quickly chip off, or may never dry properly. Also, you need to know what type of paint to use. A glossy paint in a photography studio, for instance, will reflect flashbulbs and ruin the photographs. You must know how to mix the colors of paint to match the customer's wishes or existing paint. Finally, you must evenly and neatly apply one or more coats of paint. Customers get very upset at stray dribbles of paint on their floors and bubbles and cracks in the corner! Painters use a variety of tools to apply paint, including bristle brushes, pressure brushes, and paint sprayers. Painters also sometimes stain and varnish wood.

A paperhanger's job is easier in some ways and harder in others. The wallpaper must be cut to size, and the patterns on the pieces must be matched. You must make sure the wallpaper is free from rips, tears, and other flaws. Then you must carefully apply the wallpaper, being careful to do so evenly and not to trap any air bubbles underneath.

Before painting or hanging wallpaper you must prepare your work surface. The walls must be clean. Old paint or wallpaper may need to be removed by steaming, using chemical solvents, or physically chipping or sanding it away. Holes or chips in the surface may need to be filled in. This can be strenuous work.

Who You'll Work For

✵ Homeowners looking to renovate their homes
✵ Contractors who work on residential and commercial properties
✵ Residential, commercial, and industrial construction companies
✵ City, state, and local governments

Your Typical Day

Here are the highlights of a typical day for a paperhanger.

✓ **Out with the old.** The Smith family is moving to a bigger house, and they've hired you to hang some new wallpaper to enhance their old house's market value. Before you hang the new

Let's Talk Money

The median income for painters and paperhangers is $14.55 per hour , ranging from $9.47 to $25.11, according to 2006 figures from the U.S. Bureau of Labor Statistics. Those working for local governments tend to make the most money, while those working for employment services tend to make the least. Those working in construction tend to make about the average for all painters and paperhangers.

Let's Talk Trends

The number of painters and paperhangers is expected to grow about as fast as the national average for all industries through 2014, according to the Bureau of Labor Statistics. Job prospects are expected to be excellent due to many thousands of people retiring or leaving the profession in favor of better-paying or less strenuous work.

wallpaper, though, you'll have to carefully use a wallpaper steamer to get the old wallpaper off.

✔ **Prepare your surface.** So the new wallpaper will hang neatly, you fill in holes in the old plaster and apply *sizing* (a primer and sealant) to help it stick.

✔ **Up with the new.** After carefully cutting and matching the pattern, you paste up the new wallpaper.

Where You'll Work

Painters and paperhangers can work anywhere. While some are employed by large construction companies or as maintenance workers by city and state governments, more than half of painters and paperhangers are self-employed. Many homeowners hire independent painters and paperhangers to spruce up their homes and enhance their value.

While most paperhangers work indoors, painters' work is often outdoors. As a painter, you might paint miles of fence for a giant Thoroughbred farm in Kentucky, or you might find yourself suspended from a *swing stage,* or suspended scaffold, painting a large office building. Outdoor work is seasonal, and can depend on weather. It is very difficult to paint a house in the rain! However, since painters also work indoors, this is not always as much of a problem as it can be for other building trades.

Work hours for painters and paperhangers can be irregular. Most work an average of less than 40 hours a week, but that means that you may find yourself working 60 hours one week and less than 20 the next. Some painters and paperhangers only work part-time. Some painters enhance their earnings by doing decorative work, such as murals and trim.

Though you may have to climb ladders and go up into high places, painters' work is usually not very dangerous. The one exception is in removing old lead-based paint, in which case you will need special equipment.

What You Can Do Now

✴ Learn about color theory. Some colors work well together, while others don't.

✴ Work as a painter or paperhanger's helper. You can gain valuable experience while earning money.

✴ Pay attention in school. Painters and paperhangers need to be good at math to correctly measure and cut wallpaper or estimate how much paint they will need to cover an area of wall.

What Training You'll Need

Most painters and paperhangers learn by working as helpers to more experienced laborers. There are formal apprenticeship programs that take two to four years, including 144 hours of classroom instruction per year. However, very few people go through such apprenticeship programs. Many of the same skills can be learned on the job.

Painters generally learn on the job about color theory and color harmony. Some colors work better together than others do, and some produce unexpected results when mixed. Helpers may spend a lot of time spreading drop cloths and preparing surfaces to be painted or covered with wallpaper. They also learn how to remove old paint or wallpaper with chemicals and scraping, how to mix paint, how to use painting equipment, how to erect scaffolding, how to spread paint or apply wallpaper, and how to estimate the cost of a job.

Painters may also learn how to use special equipment and procedures to remove lead paint. At one point, lead was a common ingredient in many paints. Lead not only gives a brilliant white color, but it also makes the paint dry quicker and last longer. However, lead is also very toxic, and is especially dangerous to children six and younger, affecting their mental and physical development. Before lead-based paint was banned in 1978, many children were poisoned by chips or dust from lead paint. (Lead paint is still used on highways, in industry, and by the military.) Painters' work now often includes protecting their clients by carefully removing old lead paint. This involves wearing protective equipment, putting down drop cloths and sealing the area, carefully filtering the air for dust, keeping children and pets away from the work, and using special techniques to remove the lead paint.

The Inside Scoop: Q&A

Kim Anthony
Painter
Brooklyn, New York

Q: *How did you get your job?*

A: I'm a freelancer painter and artist. I paint anything and everything, from residential and high-end commercial properties to custom finishing and restoration work. My own art is abstract painting on canvas, which I sell to private buyers. I tend to get my jobs through word of mouth, personal networking, doing good work, and online classified ads.

Q: *What do you like best about your job?*

A: I like the flexibility and freedom it affords me, and also the quick cash—not to mention pride in my work. I love what I do. It doesn't seem like the daily grind.

Q: *What's the most challenging part of your job?*

A: It's either feast or famine. When I'm in between jobs—or dealing with people who don't want to pay what the work's worth (or who don't know what they want)—it can be very difficult.

Q: *What are the keys to success as a painter?*

A: Perseverance. Do the job the best you can and follow through. Always finish what you start. Follow your heart, keep to your dreams, and be happy! Also, you should be able to say NO sometimes!

How to Talk Like a Pro

Here are a few words you'll hear as a painter or paperhanger:

✯ **Swing stage** Have you ever seen painters suspended from ropes working on a tall building? The device they sit on is called a swing stage.

✴ **Bosun's chair** For painting narrow structures where a swing stage is impractical, such as church steeples, painters use a device called a bosun's chair. The bosun's chair is so called because bosuns, the crew member in charge of rigging, used them to climb up in the masts of ships.

✴ **Sizing** Sizing is put on a wall underneath the wallpaper. It helps seal cracks, smooth irregularities, and make the wallpaper stick better.

How to Find a Job

You can find work as a painter or paperhanger (or a painter or paperhanger's helper) in a number of ways. Employment agencies can help you find some work. You can also look at the help-wanted section of newspapers. City and state governments may post employment opportunities on the Web. Best of all is asking a painter or paperhanger if he or she needs an assistant. If you don't know any painters or paperhangers personally, look in the phone book and try calling some. Some trade schools may teach more skilled work such as lead paint removal. Such schools often have job-placement programs. Formal apprenticeship programs are generally through large contractors, especially those with large union membership.

If you are a self-employed painter or paperhanger, try advertising your services in newspapers or on the Internet. Web sites such as Craigslist (http://www.craigslist.org) can be a good way to announce your availability. If you do a good job, clients will recommend you to their friends. Very often, word of mouth is the best way to find work.

Secrets for *Success*

See the suggestions below and turn to the appendix for advice on résumés and interviews.

✴ Be precise. Nobody likes a sloppy paint or wallpapering job!

✴ Be accurate in estimating the cost of work. Clients don't like it when they have to pay more than they thought they would.

Reality Check

Though you can make a decent wage as a painter or paperhanger, the work can be hard, and the hours can be irregular.

Some Other Jobs to Think About

⋆ Hazmat worker. Hazmat workers deal especially with dangerous chemicals, and can make very good money. If you have experience removing lead paint, why not do such work full time?

⋆ Carpet or tile installer. What painters and paperhangers are to walls, carpet and tile installers are to floors.

⋆ Plaster or stucco mason. Plaster and stucco masons are skilled laborers who help to put decorative finishes on walls. They are paid slightly better than painters and paperhangers.

How You Can Move Up

⋆ Go into business for yourself. More than half of painters and paperhangers are self-employed. Be an entrepreneur and start your own company.

⋆ Learn a skill. Painters who know how to remove lead paint can charge a premium for their services.

⋆ Become an interior decorator. If you have good taste, why stop at the walls? Interior decorators advise people on how to enhance their homes' beauty.

Web Sites to Surf

International Union of Painters and Allied Trades. The union for painters and other professionals, providing advocacy, scholarships, and other benefits. http://www.iupat.org

Department of Healthy Homes and Lead Hazard Control. The U.S. Department of Housing and Urban Development's page for lead-paint education. http://www.hud.gov/offices/lead

Earn a good wage

Electrician

Get a charge out of your work

Learn a valuable skill

Electrician

The ancient Greeks knew that rubbing fur with amber could produce an electric spark, but electricity (from the Greek *elektron*, or amber) wasn't identified as a natural force until the 16th century. It was not until the late-19th century that inventors such as Nikola Tesla, Samuel Morse, and Thomas Edison began devising practical uses for electricity. To a world that had been lit only by fire, electrical lights, telegraphs, and radios seemed nothing short of miraculous. Today electricity powers the computers, air conditioners, and other things that keep our economy going. Electricians are the ones who install and fix electrical wiring in homes and offices, and most electricians began as electrician's assistants. Around 656,000 electricians work in the United States today.

Is This Job for You?

To find out if being an electrician is right for you, read each of the following questions and answer "Yes" or "No."

Yes	No	**1.**	Are you extremely careful and safety conscious?
Yes	No	**2.**	Do you follow directions well?
Yes	No	**3.**	Are you very precise?
Yes	No	**4.**	Are you good with your hands?
Yes	No	**5.**	Are you good at math and science?
Yes	No	**6.**	Do you study things until you understand them?
Yes	No	**7.**	Are you not color-blind?
Yes	No	**8.**	Do you pay attention to rules?
Yes	No	**9.**	Can people depend on you?
Yes	No	**10.**	Are you good at reading blueprints and plans?

If you answered "Yes" to most of these questions, you should consider a career as an electrician. To find out more about this job, read on.

What You'll Do

Power: That's what an electrician's work is all about. Electricians install, connect, maintain, and test electrical systems for homes, offices, manufacturing plants, and everything else that needs power.

Let's Talk Money

The median income for electricians is $20.33 per hour, ranging from $12.18 to $33.64, according to 2006 figures from the U.S. Bureau of Labor Statistics. Electrician's assistants tend to make less money than licensed electricians, as they are still learning the trade. Electricians who work in automotive manufacturing tend to make the most money, and those who work for employment services make the least.

Following blueprints provided by the architect, electricians run electrical conduits or insulated wires inside walls and floors, where they are hidden and out of the way. *Conduits* are pipes made of plastic or metal that conceal and protect electrical wires. The wires are then connected to circuits, switches, circuit breakers, transformers, and other devices. In the course of installation, the electrician may need to strip, cut, connect, or solder the wires. The type of wire used depends on how it will serve. The thicker the wire, the more current it can channel.

Electricians also test wiring with tools such as ammeters and voltmeters, and ohmmeters. These measure the current traveling through the wires to ensure that they work, are safe, are properly connected, and that all the parts are compatible. Old wiring may corrode, break, or become dangerous, so an electrician needs to test and occasionally replace parts. Most maintenance is routine. For instance, old-fashioned fuse boxes may be replaced with circuit breakers. In industrial settings, electricians may be required to fix malfunctioning motors, generators, and other electrical machinery.

Since live electricity is very dangerous, electricians must be very careful and precise. They must also follow the regulations set down by the National Electric Code published by the National Fire Protection Association and also state and local building codes. Following these rules also keep electricians and those they work for safe.

Who You'll Work For

✯ Residential, commercial, and industrial building contractors
✯ Large- and small-scale manufacturers
✯ State and local governments
✯ Schools, universities, hospitals, and other institutions
✯ Experienced self-employed electricians

Where You'll Work

Electricians can work indoors or outdoors in all sorts of weather—any place where electricity is needed, including homes, factories, and construction sites. The one place where electricians don't work is in the rain or where it's wet, since this can be dangerous.

Electricians who are self-employed or who work for hourly wages, such as in construction, may have irregular work schedules. Electricians who are salaried, on the other hand, tend to work 40-hour weeks. Those who work in maintenance—or who are working on time-sensitive construction projects—may also need to work nights, weekends, or overtime. Often, large factories that run 24 hours a day employ three shifts of electricians. Electricians who work in industry may have scheduled overtime during periodic maintenance or upgrades.

Electricians' work can be strenuous, and can involve lifting heavy objects, and standing, kneeling, or lying down for long periods of time. However, as a rule, it tends to be less strenuous than that of other construction trades. The one constant is the need to pay strict attention to safety. This is both for your benefit and for the benefit of the people you work for. No one likes to be shocked by an ungrounded electrical line!

Your Typical Day

Here are the highlights of a typical day for an electrician.

- ✓ **Meet the boss.** Since you are just learning the trade you'll be working under the supervision of a more experienced electrician. You meet your boss at the job site bright and early.
- ✓ **Feed some wires.** Today you'll be wiring a new house. As your boss connects the electrical system on the other side of the living

Let's Talk Trends

According to the Bureau of Labor Statistics, the number of electricians will grow about as fast as the national average through 2014. As the economy and the demand for electrical power grows, the need for trained and skilled electricians will grow as well. Also, large numbers of electricians are expected to retire over the next decade, opening up new positions.

room wall, you run the wires to him and keep them from getting snarled together

✓ **Test it.** After painstakingly wiring the house, you test your work. The meters say everything is A-OK. Good job!

What You Can Do Now

✴ Learn all about electricity. Especially pay attention in physics and math classes.

✴ Build some models. There are many hobby kits designed to teach you about electric circuitry.

✴ Take shop classes. There are many electrical projects you can do now.

What Training You'll Need

Electricians go through some of the most rigorous training of all the construction trades. Most electricians learn through apprenticeship programs run by employers, or by unions such as the International Brotherhood of Electrical Workers, the National Electrical Contractors Association, and the Associated Builders and Contractors and the Independent Electrical Contractors Association. Most only take high school graduates 18 years of age or older, last four years, and involve at least 144 hours of classroom instruction and 2,000 hours of on-the-job training. These apprenticeship programs will qualify you to work as an electrician in both maintenance and construction. There are also many vocational and trade schools that can teach you how to become an electrician. Many employers look favorably on such programs, but you won't get to "learn while you earn," as in an apprenticeship program. Some people work as electrician's assistants before they enter an apprenticeship program or a trade or vocational school. Electrician's assistants set up sites, take care of materials, drill holes, and do other non-electrical tasks.

No matter whether you enter a trade school or an apprenticeship program, all electricians need to know the same things. You will learn electrical theory, electrical code requirements, how to read blueprints, and special skills such as how to solder or connect a fire alarm. You will learn to measure wire and conduit, install, connect, and test switches and outlets, and do all the other parts of an electrician's work.

Most local governments require electricians to be licensed. In order to pass the licensing test, you will need to know electrical theory and

The Inside Scoop: Q&A

Kenny Waite
Electrician
Straudsburg, Pennsylvania

Q: *How did you get your job?*

A: The Electrical Union used to be a father/son only union, but they decided to open to the public in the 1960s. I found out when and where to go to fill out an application and applied for the apprenticeship program.

Q: *What do you like best about your job?*

A: The field is interesting because the work varies from job to job. You're not always doing the same thing—you're working on new construction, computer wiring, data and telephone wiring, etc.

Q: *What's the most challenging part of your job?*

A: The challenges include meeting deadlines, running a crew when you are a foreman, making sure everything is done according to blueprints, plans, and the building code.

Q: *What are the keys to success as an electrician?*

A: The keys to success are true for all fields: Show up for work on time every day, get the proper training for your job, work well with people, and be happy with what you do for a living.

both national and local electric codes. You may also need to take classes throughout your career to keep abreast of the latest technology. This is not a job for people who don't like to study!

How to Talk Like a Pro

Here are a few words you'll hear as an electrician:

✦ **Voltage** Voltage is the measure of the electrical potential in an electrical network. It is the ability of an electric field to cause an electric current. If an electrical wire is a hose, then you might think of it as being like the water pressure in the hose.

✴ **Amperage** If the voltage is the potential, then the amperage is the flow of that charge—its quantity. You can think of it as the amount of water in that hose.

✴ **Ground** Also called the *earth*, this is a conductor that helps protect against faults by routing the current into the ground. You can think of it as an overflow drain for that hose.

How to Find a Job

The best way to look for an apprenticeship program is by contacting local large contractors and unions. It often helps to have a personal recommendation to get into these programs. If you choose to go to a trade or vocational school instead, many of these schools have job-placement programs that can help you find work after you graduate.

Electricians can't be hired without training. However, after your training is complete you should be able to take all sorts of jobs. Look in your local newspaper and on the Internet for help-wanted ads. Also send your résumé to the human resources departments of local companies and contractors who might employ electricians. You can often find these companies in the phone book. If you would rather freelance and hire yourself out, then newspaper ads and Web sites such as Craigslist (http://www.craigslist.org) are good ways to find clients. Perhaps best of all is the recommendation of a satisfied customer, so always do a good job!

Secrets for Success

See the suggestions below and turn to the appendix for advice on résumés and interviews.

✴ Be precise! People's safety, as well as your own, depends on your work.

✴ Pay attention in class. Electrician is perhaps the most academic of all building trades.

Reality Check

Being an electrician is a very good job. However, it can sometimes be uncomfortable or dangerous. Electricity can seriously injure or even kill you. Always be safety conscious!

Some Other Jobs to Think About

⭐ Heating, air conditioner, and refrigeration mechanic or installer. These workers must have many of the same skills as electricians.

⭐ Phone or cable installer. These jobs are much simpler than an electrician's.

⭐ Elevator installer or repairer. These skilled laborers make very high salaries.

How You Can Move Up

⭐ Get your license. In most places, a license is required to work as an electrician.

⭐ Go into business for yourself. About one in ten electricians is self-employed.

⭐ Become a supervisor. Electricians with a lot of experience can become supervisors at large companies, project managers, or inspectors.

Web Sites to Surf

U.S. Department of Labor. The Department of Labor's Occupational Outlook Handbook has many links for information about apprenticeship programs (scroll to the bottom of the page). http://www.bls.gov/oco/ocos206.htm

The National Electric Code. The National Fire Protection Association's guidelines for the industry. http://www.nfpa.org/aboutthecodes/AboutTheCodes .asp?DocNum=70&cookie%5Ftest=1

Learn a skilled trade

Plumber or Pipe Fitter

Have your skills be in demand

Make an excellent wage

Plumber or Pipe Fitter

The ancient Romans used aqueducts to supply their cities with fresh water, but from the fall of Rome up until the mid-19th century, most people lived without plumbing. Water was taken from wells, and garbage and waste was thrown in the streets or fields. While this was not so much of a problem in rural areas, cities were filthy and unhygienic. For instance, people said of 18th-century Edinburgh, Scotland, that "you smelled it before you saw it." If you take a moment to imagine modern cities without plumbing, you'll realize why plumbers' and pipe fitters' jobs are so important. These laborers do more than just install and maintain water systems, though—they also work on oil and gas lines, air-conditioning, manufacturing plants, and anywhere else where something has to be piped in or out. This makes plumbers' and pipe fitters' skills critical.

There are about 561,000 plumbers and pipe fitters working in the U.S. today. About 1 in 10 plumbers and pipe fitters are self-employed, and 1 in 3 belong to a union. Most people in the profession are men.

Is This Job for You?

To find out if being a plumber or pipe fitter is right for you, read each of the following questions and answer "Yes" or "No."

Yes	No	**1.**	Can you follow instructions carefully?
Yes	No	**2.**	Are you physically fit?
Yes	No	**3.**	Can you work as part of a team?
Yes	No	**4.**	Are you careful in your work?
Yes	No	**5.**	Do you like working with your hands?
Yes	No	**6.**	Are you careful and safety conscious?
Yes	No	**7.**	Do you always make sure a job is done right?
Yes	No	**8.**	Do you have a good work ethic?
Yes	No	**9.**	Can people count on you?
Yes	No	**10.**	Are you good at math and science?

If you answered "Yes" to most of these questions, you might want to think about a career as a plumber or pipe fitter. To find out more about these jobs, read on.

Let's Talk Money

Plumbers and pipe fitters are some of the best paid of the construction trades. The median income for plumbers and pipe fitters is $19.85 per hour, ranging from $11.62 to $33.72, according to the U.S. Bureau of Labor Statistics. Those working in the natural gas industry tend to make the most, and those working for local governments, the least. As an apprentice or trainee plumber or pipe fitter, you'll start on the lower end of the salary scale.

What You'll Do

About half of plumbers and pipe fitters are employed by contractors in the construction industry. Others work in industrial settings, power plants, and for the government. Pipe fitters, for instance, are essential in the pharmaceutical and chemical industries, where large amounts of liquids must be pumped from one place to another to synthesize drugs or other products.

Plumbers who work in construction do far more than just installing plumbing. Besides water and waste disposal systems, plumbers are often also in charge of air-conditioning, heating, gas, and drainage systems. They install fixtures such as bathtubs, toilets, sinks, showers, washing machines, and boilers, and, of course, maintain them as well (as anyone who's ever had a clogged toilet will know). Plumbers may also need to cut holes in walls and floors, cut, bend, and solder lengths of pipe, or connect sections of plastic pipe with adhesive. They need to know how to read blueprints in order to know where to install these things, and building codes to make sure that everything is up to spec in the course of their work. After installing the plumbing system, plumbers need to be able to connect it to the municipal water and gas supplies and test the system to make sure that it works.

Pipe fitters tend to work on larger-scale projects, such as the high- and low-pressure pipes used in manufacturing, municipal sewer systems, and power plants. They may also install and maintain the electronic controls for these systems. There are also sub-specialties of pipe fitting, such as *sprinkler fitters*, who specifically install automatic fire sprinklers, and *steam fitters*, who work with pipes that move high-pressure, often dangerously hot liquids and gases.

Different materials are used for different jobs. Many years ago, lead was commonly used for pipes (in fact, *plumber* comes from *plumbum*, the Latin word for lead). However, it was discovered that lead is poisonous, so copper replaced lead as the standard material for pipes. Today, plastic commonly replaces copper. Steel is usually used for heavy-duty applications.

Who You'll Work For

✴ Private individuals such as homeowners
✴ Commercial, residential, and industrial construction companies
✴ Manufacturers and industrial plants
✴ Building owners
✴ Local, state, and the federal government

Where You'll Work

Plumbers and pipe fitters can be found in homes, factories, office buildings, power plants, and other domestic and industrial settings around the country. Most plumbers and pipe fitters work 40-hour weeks. The exception is if you are employed maintaining a company's pipe systems, or by a company contracted to maintain such systems. In such a case you may need to work evenings or weekends, or be on call in case of an emergency. You may also work at two or more job sites located some distance apart.

Plumbers employed in construction may work sporadically. After a project is finished, you may spend some time out of work. However, because plumbing must always be maintained, plumbers and pipe fitters have less worries about unemployment than do people working in other construction trades.

Plumbers' and pipe fitters' work can also be strenuous. You may have to lift heavy pipes, stand, bend, stretch, kneel, or otherwise work in uncomfortable positions. You may need to work outdoors in bad weather, and there is also a danger of burning yourself on a hot pipe or otherwise being injured. This is why it is important to pay attention to safety.

Let's Talk Trends

The number of plumbers and pipe fitters will grow about as fast as the national average through 2014, and job opportunities are expected to outstrip the number of trained and qualified workers, according to the Bureau of Labor Statistics. This means that wages will be at a premium. No wonder Albert Einstein once said that if he could live his life over again, he would become a plumber!

Your Typical Day

Here are the highlights of a typical day for a plumber.

✓ **Pull it out.** The Johnson family has hired you to install their new dishwasher. First, though, you'll have to take the old one out. While crawling underneath their kitchen counters, you also discover why their waste disposal doesn't work: One of the kids dropped a toy in there!

✓ **Put it in.** The new dishwasher is pushed into position and the water lines are connected. It's important to get this right, or the Johnsons will be washing their plates with wastewater from the shower upstairs. Yuck!

✓ **Test it.** Not only does the new dishwasher work—you can see your reflection in the glasses. Good job!

What Training You'll Need

Very few plumbers and pipe fitters just "pick up" their skills. While some learn their skills informally on the job, or in the armed forces, most learn their trade from either trade and vocational schools or formal apprenticeship programs.

Though they can be difficult to get into, apprenticeship programs are generally considered to provide the best training. These are operated either by unions or by local contractor organizations. Generally, you must be 18 years old, in good physical condition, and have a high school diploma to begin an apprenticeship program. Apprenticeships generally last four to five years and include on-the-job training and 144 hours per year of classroom instruction. You will start at the bottom as a plumber's helper, unloading pipe, drilling holes, and performing other small tasks. Your instruction will include reading blueprints, local plumbing codes and regulations, identifying types of pipe and what they are used for, and on-the-job safety. You will learn to use tools, solder pipes, install plumbing, and do all the jobs that plumbers perform. At the end of your apprenticeship, you will have a thorough knowledge of all sorts of plumbing.

Trade and vocational schools also give you a very good start in this profession. Potential employers will know that you have had thorough training in plumbing. You may, however, still need to complete an apprenticeship. A company may still give you additional training in the particular layout and use of their pipe system.

The Inside Scoop: Q&A

Gershon Schapiro
Plumber
Brooklyn, New York

Q: *How did you get your job?*

A: I grew up in a family-owned plumbing and heating business and learned my trade the hard—and in my opinion the best—way: By going out with different plumbing mechanics from job to job, observing the work they did, asking questions, and participating on any level and in any way possible. Even if it meant just carrying the tool bucket, plugging in the extension, holding the tools, or just standing there doing nothing. After finishing school I decided that I wanted to stick with the trade. At first I assisted my father with whatever was necessary. Then, over time, I developed a good feeling, a sense of pride, and the satisfaction of accomplishing something with my own two hands.

Q: *What do you like best about your job?*

A: The fact that I am able to go in and help someone solve their problem or accomplish the task I set out to do with pride. I know not everyone is qualified and able to do this, so it gives me extra satisfaction that I can. I also like the fact that you can meet a great assortment of people, each with their own unique characteristics. You will be surprised what you can learn from people.

Q: *What's the most challenging part of your job?*

A: The most challenging part is when you go on a job that involves a difficult repair or takes time and effort to correctly diagnose the problem. You are challenged to correctly and efficiently correct the problem while bearing monetary or space restrictions in mind.

Q: *What are the keys to success as a plumber?*

A: (A) Honesty: This is the most important key to success. (B) Working smart, not hard. (C) Morality. For me most of it is my belief in God. I do not preach religion when I work, but I am not afraid to

(Continued on next page)

(continued from previous page)

show it. I dress like a religious Jew. I don't wear a suit and white shirt when I work, but I do wear a special four-cornered garment called tzizis, which has eight strings and five knots on each corner. I wear the strings hanging out from my pants. I am proud of who I am and only fear God and respect my elders.

Most communities require plumbers to be licensed, though there are no uniform national standards. Generally, you will have to pass a test that will ensure you have a thorough knowledge of the trade and the local laws.

What You Can Do Now

✯ Learn all you can about plumbing. There are many "how-to" books for home-fix-it types.

✯ Research trade schools and apprenticeship programs. Good training is necessary to become a plumber or pipe fitter.

✯ Pay attention in math, science, and technical drawing classes. These will help you with the skills you need.

How to Talk Like a Pro

Here are a few words you'll hear as a plumber or pipe fitter:

✯ **PVC** Polyvinyl chloride, a type of plastic often used for plumbing. It is cheap, flexible, and durable. However, because it gives off toxic fumes when it is burned, PVC is banned in some municipalities.

✯ **NPT** National Pipe Thread, the standard thread gauges for pipes in the United States.

✯ **DWS** Domestic Water System—the water system in a house, including the fresh water intake and wastewater outlet.

How to Find a Job

The best way to look for an apprenticeship program is to contact local unions and large contractors. It often helps to have a personal recommendation to get into these programs. A good work or military record also helps. If you choose to go to a trade or vocational school instead, many of these schools have job-placement programs that can help you find work or an apprenticeship program after you graduate.

Although plumbers and pipe fitters can't be hired without training, afterward you should be able to take all sorts of jobs. Look in your local newspaper and on the Internet for help-wanted ads. Also send your résumé to the human resources departments of local manufacturers, construction companies, and contractors who might employ plumbers and pipe fitters. You can often find these companies in the phone book. If you would rather freelance and hire yourself out, then you can take out newspaper ads and post your availability on Web sites such as Craigslist (http://www.craigslist.org). Perhaps best way of all to find a job is word of mouth. Make sure that anyone you have worked for can give you a good recommendation.

Secrets for Success

See the suggestions below and turn to the appendix for advice on résumés and interviews.

- ✴ Always be precise and do a good job. Remember, people are counting on your work!
- ✴ Try to estimate costs correctly. Customers don't like having to pay much more than they originally anticipated.

Reality Check

Plumbing and pipe fitting can be strenuous and demanding. However, they are also very well-paid careers. Very few workers in this field are unhappy with their work!

Some Other Jobs to Think About

- ✴ Heating, air conditioner, and refrigeration mechanic or installer. These workers must have many of the same skills as plumbers and pipe fitters.
- ✴ Industrial machinery installation and repair. You will be doing much the same thing as an industrial pipe fitter, but with even more specialized skills.
- ✴ Electrician. Just like plumbers and pipe fitters, electricians are essential to construction,

How You Can Move Up

⭐ Become a construction manager. Plumbers can move up to supervise other construction workers, especially in jobs requiring their specialized skills.

⭐ Become an inspector. Plumbing inspectors must have a thorough knowledge of the trade, as well as local codes and regulations.

⭐ Go into business for yourself. Independent plumbers get to set their own hours and take the jobs they want!

Web Sites to Surf

United Association of Journeymen and Apprentices of the Plumbing and Pipe Fitting Industry. Information on apprenticeships. http://www.ua.org

ThePlumber.com. Everything you've ever wanted to know about plumbing, and some things you probably didn't. http://www.theplumber.com

Make something lasting

Cement or Brick Mason

Pour yourself into your work

See your finished product take shape

Cement or Brick Mason

What do the great buildings of ancient Rome have in common with the suburban patio? They're all made of cement and bricks! Cement and brick are two of the oldest building materials known, and people who are skilled in working with them are as much in demand today as they were in ancient times. (Of course, cement and brick masons are paid a bit better today than they were in ancient Rome—the Romans built their monuments with slave labor!) Cement can be used for making everything from sidewalks and floors to huge dams, and brick can make homes and offices. As either a cement or brick mason, you'll have the satisfaction of knowing you've created something that will last for years. Today there are about 209,000 cement masons and 177,000 brick masons working in the United States. More men than women tend to work in this field.

Is This Job for You?

To find out if being a cement or brick mason is right for you, read each of the following questions and answer "Yes" or "No."

Yes No **1.** Do you like working with your hands?

Yes No **2.** Do you like to feel a sense of accomplishment in your work?

Yes No **3.** Can you lift heavy loads?

Yes No **4.** Are you precise and do you pay attention to details?

Yes No **5** Can you pay attention to directions?

Yes No **6.** Do you like to build things?

Yes No **7.** Are you in good physical shape?

Yes No **8.** Are you good at math?

Yes No **9.** Do you like working with tools?

Yes No **10.** Are you careful and safety-conscious?

If you answered "Yes" to most of these questions, you might be right for a career as a cement or brick mason. To find out more about these jobs, read on.

Let's Talk Money

The median income for cement masons is $15.10 per hour and $20.07 for brick masons, ranging from $9.53 to $20.89 for cement masons and from $11.68 to $30.43 for brick masons, according to 2006 figures from the U.S. Bureau of Labor Statistics. Wages vary depending on where you work, what company you work for, and how long you've been a mason. Overtime pay can increase your earnings significantly, but it can also be hard to find work in the winter. Benefits are usually supplied by employers or the International Union of Bricklayers and Allied Craftworkers.

What You'll Do

Cement and brick masons build everything from front walks to huge office buildings and public works projects. The work can be physically demanding, requiring long hours, heavy lifting and bending, and working in cramped positions.

Brick masons put bricks or concrete blocks in place, alternating bricks with mortar to make a strong wall. There are two methods of building a masonry wall. One is called the *corner lead*, and the other is the *corner pole*. In the corner lead, experienced masons will build a *lead*, or pyramid of bricks, in the corner, while others will fill in the wall. Because this is difficult and time-consuming, masons will sometimes use corner poles (also called *masonry guides*) to make sure their walls line up. Either method requires precise work and careful attention to the building plans. Mistakes can be very costly.

Concrete, which is a mixture of sand, gravel, water, and Portland cement (a binding agent), can be very difficult to work with, since it hardens quickly. (Portland cement does not come from Portland, Oregon. Rather, it was named after its similarity to Portland stone, which was widely used for building in 19th-century Britain.) Cement masons first make the forms into which the concrete is poured. They then level and smooth it with shovels and a tool called a *bull float*. For a nonslip surface, the surface of the concrete is brushed. To prevent cracking, a tool called a *groover* is used to make lines. Cement masons can also do decorative work, such as *terrazzo*, in which different-colored stones are pressed into the cement to make a picture or design, and *aggregate*, in which small stones are left on the surface of the cement. Cement masons must have a good knowledge of concrete

Let's Talk Trends

The job outlook for cement masons is expected to be good, and that for brick masons very good, through 2014; job growth for both should be in-line with all other occupations, according to the Bureau of Labor Statistics. Because of the strenuous and skilled nature of the work, there is both high turnover and a demand for experienced workers.

chemistry, so that they know how quickly the concrete will harden. No one wants a half-filled concrete form—or, worse, a cement truck full of hardened concrete!

Who You'll Work For

✶ Construction companies

✶ Government agencies

✶ General contractors

✶ Business and home owners

Where You'll Work

Cement and brick masons tend to work outdoors both in the cold of winter and in the heat of summer—though there tends to be less work in the winter. This can affect your earnings, though in areas of the country where the weather is generally good, such as the South and Southwest, cement and brick masons can work year-round. Work also tends to stop in bad weather, though new materials are allowing masons to work in all sorts of conditions. Some of the work, such as making terrazzo floors, is indoors.

The sorts of places you may work are as varied as the buildings you'll make. One day you may be making a new deck for someone's house, while another you'll be making a sidewalk for a shopping center or a wall for a government building. About one out of every three brick masons is self-employed, mainly doing small-scale work such as home renovations. On the other hand, because of the expensive equipment involved in the work, such as cement mixers, very few cement masons are self-employed—about 1 out of 20. Most work for general contractors or large construction companies, and a few work for companies that make cement or cement-related products. The sort of work you'll do may depend on what sort of company you work for: Small contractors are not often hired for big government projects, and large construction companies don't often make backyard patios.

The Inside Scoop: Q&A

Daniel Bozman
Cement mason
Peoria, Illinois

Q: *How did you get your job?*

A: It was pretty easy—I was dating my employer's niece. She introduced me to him one afternoon, and he hired me the next day. It's kind of like what you'll hear a lot in life—"It's not what you know, it's who you know."

Q: *What do you like best about your job?*

A: I get to work outside, and every day is something different—different job locations, different tasks, etc. I also like that you can make good money at it, and it keeps me in really good shape, so long as I eat right and drink lots of water.

Q: *What's the most challenging part of your job?*

A: The most challenging, I'd have to say, would be keeping the concrete flat and staying ahead of it and the sun (that is, finishing it before it's too hard). I'd also say that it's pretty challenging working around the weather sometimes. Since you can't pour concrete in the rain, you almost need to be a weatherman too, some days.

Q: *What are the keys to success as a cement mason?*

A: Good management, good equipment, a hard-working crew, and quality craftsmanship.

Your Typical Day

Here are the highlights of a typical day for a cement mason.

- ✓ **Wake up early.** The weatherman says that it's going to rain in the afternoon. Your boss says to get to the job site early so that the concrete will have time to set.
- ✓ **Pour it out.** The cement truck is delayed by traffic, so when it arrives, you and your coworkers quickly get to work pouring out the concrete before it sets and ruins the truck's barrel.

✔ **Smooth it out.** Now that you've gotten the cement out of the truck, you've got to quickly spread it out and smooth it down. Just as it finishes setting, the rain starts. You've finished just in time!

What You Can Do Now

⭐ Learn about building trades by talking to people who work as masons. Contacts in the business can also help you find jobs.

⭐ Find an apprenticeship program. Many companies and unions run training programs for people who want to become cement and brick masons. Also, with an apprenticeship program, you can be paid while you lean a trade.

⭐ Study your math and chemistry. Brick and cement masons need to be good at geometry and problem solving, while cement masons must also know the properties of concrete.

What Training You'll Need

Most cement and brick masons learn their jobs informally. Many masons begin as construction workers. Some work as assistants to more experienced masons, learning on the job. Others join two-, three-, or four-year apprenticeship programs. These programs are run by local companies, trade associations, or the International Union of Bricklayers and Allied Craftworkers. Trainees begin with simple jobs, such as smoothing the edges of poured concrete, mixing mortar, and moving molds before gradually moving to more difficult tasks. Brick masons who work for large contractors, with more varied work, will tend to learn the most. Because smaller companies tend to take smaller and simpler projects, such as home renovation, masons who work for such companies tend to learn less because there is not as much variety within or between jobs.

These are not trades for people who don't like using their heads! Apprentice masons receive classroom instruction—144 recommended hours per year for brick masons. You will learn how to read blueprints, sketch plans, and lay out work. Paying attention in school is also very important for becoming a brick mason or cement mason. Algebra can help you figure out how much cement to mix. Chemistry will teach you how raw ingredients combine to become cement. Geometry and mathematics will help you align walls and build straight lines, as well as figure out how much a job will cost. Shop class will also get you used to using tools and being safety-conscious.

In general, you will need to be at least 17 years old to become a brick mason and 18 to become a cement mason. In both cases, you will need to be in good physical shape. It will also help to have a driver's license.

How to Talk Like a Pro

Here are a few words you'll hear as a cement or brick mason:

- ✴ **Corner lead** The corner of a wall, built first to guide the laying of the rest of the wall.
- ✴ **Bull float** A tool for smoothing poured concrete.
- ✴ **Portland cement** A mixture of calcium, silicon, and aluminum oxides that forms the binding agent in most concrete.

How to Find a Job

One way to find a job as a cement or brick mason is by contacting employers directly. Because employers generally train cement and brick masons on the job, they are often willing to take inexperienced workers. Help-wanted ads are another way of finding a job, as is asking people you know who work in construction. If a personal contact is willing to vouch for you as a hard worker, it can open many doors. Some technical schools also offer courses in cement and brick masonry.

Many cement and brick masons begin as construction workers. Consider starting at the bottom. Once you've shown your employers that you're a hard worker, ask how you can be trained as a cement or brick mason.

Also consider asking the International Union of Bricklayers and Allied Craftworkers for job leads in your area. Once you find a job, you can join the union yourself. Though not all cement and brick masons belong to the union, it can provide many benefits, such as minimum wages, job placement, and health, unemployment, and accident insurance.

Secrets for Success

See the following suggestions and turn to the appendix for advice on résumés and interviews.

✯ Pay close attention to detail. It is easy to ruin expensive work through a moment's inattention. This includes being aware of safety issues. Proper attention to possible hazards prevents accidents!

✯ Become a master of organization. Every job you work on will go smoother if you do.

Reality Check

Masonry is hard, demanding physical work. You will be lifting, bending, and straining outdoors in all sorts of weather. It can also be dangerous if you're not careful.

Some Other Jobs to Think About

✯ Construction worker. You may have to spend time doing work as an ordinary construction worker before your employer allows you to apprentice as a mason.

✯ Carpet installer. Carpet is much softer than bricks or cement—but a roll of carpet can be heavy as well!

✯ Carpenters. Carpenters are skilled craftspeople who work with wood, rather than stone, concrete, or cement, but much the same skills apply.

How You Can Move Up

✯ Become an inspector. Building inspectors need to have a thorough knowledge of what they're inspecting—and the work is much less demanding!

✯ Learn a specialty. For instance, *refractory masons* specialize in installing special tiles in steel mills.

✯ Go into business for yourself. Once you've been working for a few years and saved up some money, why not begin your own contracting company?

Web Sites to Surf

International Union of Bricklayers and Allied Craftworkers. The union's Web site, including the BAC Job Network.   http://www.bacweb.org

Concrete Decor Magazine. Learn about the latest techniques for fine decorative concrete masonry.   http://www.concretedecor.net

Learn on the job

Carpet Installer

Make homes and offices beautiful

Work in a recession-proof trade

Great Careers

Carpet Installer

Carpets were invented in Central Asia 5,000 years ago. By the 10th century, they had reached Moorish Spain. The carpets brought back to Europe by the Crusaders usually were used on walls or tables, and it was not until the 18th century that they began to be commonly used on floors. In the beginning, carpets were made from wool by hand and were very expensive, but modern materials and manufacturing has made it easier and cheaper to make all sorts of carpets from oriental rugs to deep-pile shag. Today carpet is one of the most common floor coverings, adding beauty and value to homes and offices. There are 184,000 carpet and tile installers in the United States. Almost half are self-employed.

Is This Job for You?

To find out if being a carpet installer is right for you, read each of the following questions and answer "Yes" or "No."

Yes	No	**1.**	Are you a careful and precise worker?
Yes	No	**2.**	Can you lift and carry heavy loads?
Yes	No	**3.**	Are you patient and do you plan carefully?
Yes	No	**4.**	Can you follow directions?
Yes	No	**5.**	Do you have a good eye for color?
Yes	No	**6.**	Are you in good physical shape?
Yes	No	**7.**	Do you like working with your hands?
Yes	No	**8.**	Can you work as part of a team?
Yes	No	**9.**	Are you good at math and geometry?
Yes	No	**10.**	Are you not afraid of hard work?

If you answered "Yes" to most of these questions, you might want to consider a career as a carpet installer. To find out more about this job, read on.

Let's Talk Money

The median income for carpet installers is $16.39 per hour, ranging from $9.16 to $29.27. Carpet installers can also be paid by the area of carpet they install. Trainees tend to make half of what an experienced worker does.

Let's Talk Trends

The number of carpet installers is predicted to grow about as fast as the national average through 2014, according to the Bureau of Labor Statistics. More and more structures that need to be carpeted are being built, and worn-out old carpeting will need to be replaced.

What You'll Do

Carpet installing is not as simple as it sounds. First you need to inspect the surface of the floor where the carpet will go. If there are imperfections that would show through the carpet or cause the carpet to wear unevenly, you may need to correct them. You may also wish to put down some sort of padding, especially over concrete floors and other hard surfaces. Then you must measure the area to be carpeted. Because most carpet comes in 12-foot widths, you will need to cut and join the pieces of carpeting. Careful measuring and planning is important.

Carpet can be installed both with and without tacks. On special jobs, such as carpeting stairs, you may also use staples, and in commercial spaces, you may glue the carpeting directly to the floor or the padding. If you are not using tacks, then tackless strips are placed next to the walls. The carpet is then rolled out, measured, marked, and cut with a carpet knife. The carpet is positioned with a tool called a *knee kicker* and stretched to fit evenly and snugly, with a two- to three-inch margin. A *power stretcher* then stretches the carpet to lie evenly. Seams are joined with heat tape, which is a special plastic tape that is joined by heat. Finally, the edges are finished with a wall trimmer.

Who You'll Work For

* Commercial, residential, and industrial contractors and construction companies
* Home furnishings stores, including "superstores"
* Self-employment and other self-employed carpet installers

Where You'll Work

Carpet installers work in homes, offices, schools, retail establishments, restaurants, and anywhere else high-comfort, low-maintenance floor coverings are needed. Most of the work, of course, is indoors. Most carpet installers also work regular daytime hours, except for when carpet needs to be replaced after business hours in stores and other businesses. In these cases, you may need to work nights or weekends.

Carpet installation is usually one of the last steps in construction, when buildings are almost finished, so you won't need to put up with the dust and noise that other construction workers deal with. However, carpet installing can still be strenuous—carrying heavy rolls of carpet, spreading them out, reaching, bending, and kneeling. On the whole, though, carpet installation is much safer than other construction jobs.

Your Typical Day

Here are the highlights of a typical day for a carpet installer.

✓ **Pull it up.** The Murphys have decided to re-carpet their rumpus room. First, though, their hideous old carpet needs to go! Using a scraper and other tools, you pull up their old carpet and throw it in the trash.

✓ **Measure it out.** The Murphys' basement is L-shaped, so you'll need to measure carefully. After putting down some padding over the concrete floor, you cut the carpet you've brought to fit.

✓ **Tack it in.** Since the Murphys don't want carpet tacks sticking their feet, you use tackless carpet. Using the knee kicker and power spreader, you lay the carpet out and join the pieces with heat tape. Then you press it so it is secured by tackless strips and trim it. Job finished!

What Training You'll Need

Though there are a few apprenticeship programs, most carpet installers learn on the job. Mostly they are taught by more experienced professionals. Workers begin with simple work, such as stripping old carpet, stretching new carpet, and installing padding. With experience, you will be allowed to measure and cut carpet.

Meanwhile, pay attention in school. Mathematics and geometry are very important to carpet installers, both in order to measure the amount of carpet that will be needed and to estimate job costs. It also helps to be able to communicate well in Spanish, since many people working in this industry are native Spanish speakers.

The Inside Scoop: Q&A

Bob Bramlett
Carpet installer
Norfolk, Virginia

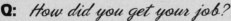

Q: *How did you get your job?*

A: I have a friend who owns a business, so one day he asked me to help out. He taught me how to do it.

Q: *What do you like best about your job?*

A: Hmm, I really don't know about a "best" part of the job. There's certainly a sense of accomplishment at the end of the day, though.

Q: *What's the most challenging part of your job?*

A: There's a lot to complain about—a lot of heavy lifting, a lot of cuts and pokes. Also, it is terrible on the knees!

Q: *What are the keys to success as a carpet installer?*

A: Just work hard. The faster you work, the more money you make!

What You Can Do Now

⭐ Pay attention in school. Carpet installers need to be good at math and geometry to lay out carpet and estimate costs.

⭐ See if you can find part-time work helping at a carpet installation business.

⭐ Get your driver's license. If you open your own business, you'll need some way of getting yourself and your material to work.

How to Talk Like a Pro

Here are a few words you'll hear as a carpet installer:

⭐ **Knee kicker** Though it looks like something you'd find on a weight machine, a knee kicker is used to position a carpet.

⭐ **Power stretcher** Any room over 10 feet by 10 feet needs to be power stretched. A power stretcher connects to the opposite wall to stretch the wrinkles out of a carpet.

✴ **Heat tape** A special adhesive tape for connecting carpet seams. It is activated by a carpet iron.

How to Find a Job

Since most carpet installers are trained on the job, people wanting to learn this trade should find employment right away. One way to find a carpet installer to work for is to look at the help-wanted section of newspapers. City and state governments may post employment opportunities on the Web. Best of all is asking a carpet installer if he or she needs an assistant. If you don't know any carpet installers personally, ask around your neighborhood and look in the phone book and try calling some. Home renovation stores also sometimes employ carpet installers.

You might also wind up working for another carpet installer, since almost half of carpet installers are self-employed. If you have the skills and want to try branching out on your own, try advertising your services in newspapers or on the Internet. Web sites such as Craigslist (http://www.craigslist.org) can be a good way to announce your availability. If you do a good job installing carpet, clients will recommend you to their friends. Very often, word of mouth is the best way to find work.

Secrets for Success

See the suggestions below and turn to the appendix for advice on résumés and interviews.

✴ Be precise and neat in your work. Carpet is supposed to make a room look better, not worse!

✴ Learn to estimate accurately the time it will take you to complete specific tasks. Effective time management is essential to working well with other people.

Reality Check

Carpet installation can be strenuous. You may have to bend, stretch, kneel, and kick the knee kicker. On the other hand, you also get to be your own boss.

Some Other Jobs to Think About

⭐ Painter or paperhanger. Work on the walls, rather than the floors.

⭐ Cement or brick mason. Make the floors, instead of covering them.

⭐ Carpenter. Like carpet installers, carpenters work with careful measurements and tools.

How You Can Move Up

⭐ Become a salesperson. Selling carpet to people is much easier— and more lucrative—than installing it!

⭐ Work your way up. Carpet installers can work their way up to become managers for big installation firms.

⭐ Start your own business. By becoming an entrepreneur, you can work for yourself!

Web Sites to Surf

Floor Covering Installation Contractors' Association. The national contractors' association. http://www.fcica.com

Carpet Guru's Carpet College. All about carpet installation and some common scams. http://www.carpetguru.com

Earn a good salary

HVAC Technician

Perform a vital service

Learn a skilled trade

HVAC Technician

HVAC—short for heating, ventilation, and air-conditioning—is a critical service. Without climate control, our modern lifestyle wouldn't exist. Productivity would crash to almost nothing in the summer, and we would still wear heavy clothes indoors all winter. Working in Manhattan high-rise office buildings in August or keeping perishable foods and medicines from spoiling would be impossible, and much of the South and Southwest would still be sparsely populated. Thanks to central heat and air-conditioning, though, the American economy can remain strong year-round. The people who maintain these critical services are HVAC technicians. There are about 270,000 HVAC technicians working in the United States. About 15 percent are self-employed.

Is This Job for You?

To find out if being an HVAC technician is right for you, read each of the following questions and answer "Yes" or "No."

Yes	No	**1.**	Do you pay attention to directions?
Yes	No	**2.**	Do you work well with other people?
Yes	No	**3.**	Are you good with tools?
Yes	No	**4.**	Are you not afraid of heights?
Yes	No	**5.**	Can you lift heavy loads?
Yes	No	**6.**	Are you in good physical condition?
Yes	No	**7.**	Are you good at math and geometry?
Yes	No	**8.**	Can you read blueprints?
Yes	No	**9.**	Do you not mind working irregular hours?
Yes	No	**10.**	Do you have a technical mind?

If you answered "Yes" to most of these questions, you should consider a career as an HVAC technician. To find out more about this job, read on.

What You'll Do

HVAC technicians install, repair, and maintain heating, ventilation, and air-conditioning systems. This can be a very complex job, requiring knowledge of gas systems, furnaces, hot-water boilers, air-conditioning units, electrical wiring, environmental regulations, building codes, and many other details. An HVAC system can include motors, compressors, fans, ducts, and various electrical components. You will need to know how each part works, what can go wrong with it, and how it fits into the overall system. Sometimes system controls must be adjusted, and sometimes broken parts must be replaced.

Routine maintenance, such as replacing filters, must also be done on a regular basis. In fact, many HVAC technicians specialize, concentrating on either maintenance and repair or installation. Some limit themselves to even more specialized fields, such as industrial refrigeration. HVAC technicians who work in maintenance may either work directly for a building owner or for a company that provides service contracts to building owners.

Either way, you will need to know how to follow blueprints and plans to install heating and air-conditioning systems, attach fuel and water supply lines, ducts, and wiring. You must also know how to check how the system is working with meters that test the amount of certain gases in the air. Incomplete combustion, or a carbon monoxide leak, can be very dangerous. You must also know how to comply with environmental regulations by conserving and recycling refrigerant gases such as chlorofluorocarbons (CFCs) and hydrochlorofluorocarbons. These gases, if allowed to escape, can be very harmful to the environment.

Who You'll Work For

★ Private building owners

★ HVAC installation companies

★ Manufacturers, factories, and other businesses that use HVAC systems

★ Federal, state, and local governments

Let's Talk Money

The median income for HVAC technicians is $17.43 per hour, ranging from $10.88 to $27.11, according to the U.S. Bureau of Labor Statistics. Those who work for supply wholesalers tend to make the most money. Apprentices tend to start off at about half the regular salary.

Let's Talk Trends

According to the Bureau of Labor Statistics, the number of HVAC technicians will grow faster than the national average through 2014. Job prospects are excellent, not only because of the retirement of many HVAC technicians, but also because of the growing need for, and complexity of, HVAC systems.

Where **You'll Work**

An HVAC technician can work anywhere there is a heating or air-conditioning system, be it a home, office, store, public building, or factory. Usually, of course, the work is indoors, but that doesn't mean that it's always comfortable. If the HVAC technician is there, it's probably because there's something wrong—such as the air conditioner not working on the hottest day of the year or the heating system failing in January. In order to fix the problem, the HVAC technician may need to bend, stretch, kneel, strain, or wedge him- or herself into a tight place.

Some of the work can be dangerous, since an HVAC technician deals with both electricity and dangerous chemicals, such as refrigerants. It is also possible to cut yourself, drop something heavy, or pull a muscle. HVAC work can be very demanding! Overall, though, it is much safer than many other construction trades.

HVAC technicians sometimes get to work only a 40-hour week, but during peak seasons, they may need to work overtime or at strange hours. Even during the summer, heating systems still need to be maintained, and the same thing goes for air-conditioning in the winter. Maintenance is best done on weekends or evenings, when occupants are away from the building and won't be interrupted in their work. Though it means long hours, this constant need for labor to keep HVAC systems running is overall a good thing since employment for HVAC technicians remains stable through the year.

Your **Typical Day**

Here are the highlights of a typical day for an HVAC technician.

✔ **Who ya gonna call?** The call comes in at 9 a.m. It's the hottest day of the year, and the air-conditioning system in one of downtown's largest office buildings has broken!

✔ **Check it out.** After crawling around in some very hot ductwork, you find the source of the problem: The system was run at such a high output, its circuits have burned out. You'll have to fix them.

✔ **Fire it up!** With the problem fixed, you start the air-conditioning up again. A lot of very sweaty office workers are very grateful to you.

What Training You'll Need

While some HVAC technicians learn the job informally, there are also many training programs and apprenticeships. Such programs are valuable because they show an employer that you know how to do the job well and have a thorough knowledge of HVAC systems. Some ways to get training are in technical high schools, trade and technical schools, and junior colleges. The armed forces also have programs in HVAC technology. Such programs usually last from six months to two years. You will study not just how to install, maintain, and repair various sorts of HVAC systems, but also the theory—what makes them work.

Apprenticeship programs are run by contractors and unions working in cooperation. They generally last from three to five years and combine practical, on-the-job training with classroom instruction in subjects such as safety practices, blueprint reading, and the theory of how heating, ventilation, and air-conditioning systems work. Math and reading skills are critical. At the end of an apprenticeship program, workers are considered fully qualified HVAC technicians.

HVAC technicians who start on the job generally assist qualified, experienced technicians. They may begin with simple jobs like carrying parts, insulating lines, or cleaning. They will learn more tasks as they progress. It is still helpful, however, to know the theory and physics of how such systems work. Self-study programs and Internet courses are becoming more popular.

In addition to job training, you may also need to pass certification exams. Technicians who work with refrigerants need to earn special certificates in one or more of the three types of certification (small appliances, high-pressure refrigerants, and low-pressure refrigerants). Such exams are given by trade schools, unions, contractor associations, or other organizations that have been approved by the Environmental Protection Agency. The industry has also developed a series of exams to certify HVAC technicians both in basic competency in residential or commercial heating and cooling and in commercial

The Inside Scoop: Q&A

Noel Nevin, 40
HVAC technician
Bronx, New York

Q: *How did you get your job?*

A: I got the job through a friend. I was going to school at night, and when there was an open position as an HVAC apprentice at the university, I knew I would get free tuition. I was going to go to grad school, in fact, but I didn't want to take a pay cut!

Q: *What do you like best about your job?*

A: You get to fix things and you've accomplished something. You've got to think it through, read the drawings, and figure out what's going on. There's a sense of accomplishment from that.

Q: *What's the most challenging part of your job?*

A: You work either on very hot or very cold equipment. If you're repairing something in the summer, it's too hot, and if you're repairing it in the winter, it's freezing. There's always a lot of noise, and it's wet and humid.

Q: *What are the keys to success as an HVAC technician?*

A: Hard work! And, of course, you have to study. But if you're willing to work, you'll do well.

refrigeration, and in working with specific equipment, such as oil-burning furnaces.

What You Can Do Now

✴ Pay attention in school. HVAC technicians need to be good at math, physics, electronics, and shop.

✴ Get a good background in electrical systems. Knowing how to safely wire a system is critical to this job.

✴ Research trade schools and apprenticeship programs.

How to Talk Like a Pro

Here are a few words you'll hear as an HVAC technician:

✴ **Carbon monoxide** An odorless, colorless, but deadly gas that can be produced by a malfunctioning furnace.

✴ **BTU** British Thermal Units, used to describe the heating and cooling power of an HVAC system.

✴ **SEER** Along with the BTU power rating, the SEER, or Seasonal Energy Efficiency Ratio, describes how energy-efficient an air conditioner is.

How to Find a Job

HVAC technicians who go through formal apprenticeship programs or technical schools have great advantages in that such programs often help place graduates in jobs. Another way to find work is to ask HVAC contractors about any job openings as an assistant or apprenticeships. Having a résumé prepared that emphasizes your strengths is a good first step toward landing such a position. You can also post your résumé in online job market sites or on community bulletin boards such as Craigslist (http://www.craigslist.org). Finally, it helps to ask people who are already certified and working as HVAC technicians if they know of any job openings.

Fully certified HVAC technicians have an easier time on the job market. They can often find openings in newspaper classified sections, making inquires of and sending résumés to contractors and building management companies, or by asking contacts in the industry. Freelance jobs can also often be found online on such forums as Craigslist.

Secrets for Success

See the suggestions below and turn to the appendix for advice on résumés and interviews.

✴ Always be thorough in your work. People's safety often relies on your expertise.

✴ Read the blueprints, and then read them again. There's nothing worse than having to redo a job.

Reality Check

Being an HVAC technician can be hard or uncomfortable work. However, the job pays very well, and HVAC technicians are rarely out of work.

Some Other Jobs to Think About

✯ Electrician. Like HVAC technicians, electricians must be technically skilled and up-to-date with codes and regulations.

✯ Home appliance repairers. Home appliance repairers must understand how things work, but do not require as extensive certification.

✯ Plumbers and pipe fitters. Also like HVAC technicians, plumbers and pipe fitters must understand duct and pipe systems, but the work is not quite as technical.

How You Can Move Up

✯ Get certified. HVAC technicians who earn certificates in specific technologies earn higher wages.

✯ Become a manager. From being an HVAC technician, you can become an HVAC supervisor, or even move into sales and marketing.

✯ Start your own business. With HVAC technicians being in such high demand, you can even start your own contracting business.

Web Sites to Surf

Air Conditioning Contractors of America. "The Contractor's Knowledge Source," containing everything from technical advice to management tips. http://www.acca.org

HVAC Excellence. A not-for-profit corporation created to help HVAC technicians "become the best they can be." http://www.hvacexcellence.org

Enter into a high-paid career

Hazmat Worker

Help protect people, homes, and businesses

Work in an exciting and necessary filed

Hazmat Worker

The results of modern industry and technology are not always beneficial. As people are coming to understand, our modern lifestyle often leaves toxic chemicals and materials as byproducts. Dangerous substances are also needed to manufacture everything from medicines to building materials. Sometimes there are accidents and these materials spill or escape into the environment. With the growing consciousness of the harmful effects of hazardous materials on people and wildlife, there has been a movement to make companies and the government responsible for cleaning up these threats to our well-being.

The threat of natural disasters and nuclear, biological, or chemical terrorism has also meant that the United States has to be prepared to deal with any emergency that may arise. This is why the jobs of hazardous materials removal and environmental cleanup workers (also called hazmat workers) are so necessary. There are about 38,000 hazardous materials removal and environmental cleanup workers in the United States today, but the number is likely to increase quickly.

Is This Job for You?

To find out if being a hazardous materials or environmental cleanup worker is right for you, read each of the following questions and answer "Yes" or "No."

Yes No **1.** Are you physically strong and in good shape?

Yes No **2.** Are you brave?

Yes No **3.** Can you lift heavy loads?

Yes No **4.** Do you always follow directions?

Yes No **5.** Can you work as part of a team?

Yes No **6.** Are you a careful and precise worker?

Yes No **7.** Do you pay attention to rules?

Yes No **8.** Are you good at math and science?

Yes No **9.** Are you good with machines and technology?

Yes No **10.** Are you not afraid of hard work?

If you answered "Yes" to most of these questions, you might want to consider a career as a hazardous materials or environmental cleanup worker. To find out more, read on.

Let's Talk Money

According to 2006 figures from the U.S. Bureau of Labor Statistics, the median income for hazardous materials and environmental cleanup workers is $16.02, ranging from $10.48 to $27.25. Treatment and disposal workers tend to be amongst the best paid, and those working with radioactive materials make even more.

What You'll Do

Hazardous materials and environmental cleanup workers work in a wide variety of situations and with a wide variety of materials. The contaminated place may be a building, vehicle, or an outdoor area in a city or in the countryside. The contaminating material may be solid, liquid, or gas, and may be dangerous for its explosive, flammable, radioactive, corrosive, reactive, or toxic properties. Cleanup and removal workers may also work with infectious agents, such as anthrax, or at treatment plants and facilities designed to store or destroy hazardous substances. The tools they use range from brooms to suits with self-contained air supplies.

Cleanup operations are always highly structured. Some are planned for years. Workers seek to identify, isolate, and contain the dangerous material and then to transport it to a safe location. However, within these guidelines, there are many varieties of work. *Emergency and disaster response* workers, for instance, respond to sudden and unexpected problems, such as spills that occur in transporting hazardous materials. They would be the first called in the event of a natural disaster that released hazardous material or a terrorist attack that used nuclear, biological, or chemical weapons. They may also have to decontaminate people affected by such a spill or attack. *Asbestos and lead abatement* workers deal with hazards in public places. Asbestos, a naturally occurring mineral, and lead paint were once widely used in buildings. Today we know that both are harmful to people's health. Abatement workers must use vacuums and other tools to clean out these materials without spreading them. About 1 in 20 hazardous materials and environmental cleanup workers works in this field. A related and growing area is *mold abatement*, which cleans potentially toxic mold out of homes and businesses. *Decommissioning and decontamination* workers deal with the radioactive materials made by nuclear facilities. They break down and contain these materials so that they can be transported to storage sites.

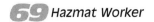

These sites are where *treatment, storage, and disposal* workers burn, bury, store, or chemically transform hazardous materials.

Who You'll Work For

✯ City, state, and the federal government
✯ Private contractors who subcontract from government agencies

Where You'll Work

Hazardous materials are, by definition, dangerous. This can make hazardous materials and environmental cleanup workers' jobs stressful. However, steps are usually taken to minimize the danger. Jobs are planned in detail, and every precaution is taken.

Outside of that, the jobs are endlessly varied. You may work indoors or outdoors, in homes, businesses and factories, or in industrial facilities and power plants. The job may require the use of hand tools or power machinery such as bulldozers. It may also require carrying heavy loads, wearing uncomfortable protective gear, or standing, stooping, or kneeling. While many hazardous materials and environmental cleanup workers work standard 40-hour weeks, overtime and weekends are often required. Other hazardous material and environmental cleanup workers must work odd hours, especially in structures that are being used. For instance, cleaning projects such as asbestos abatement often require night and weekend work.

The employment situation for hazardous materials and environmental cleanup workers is changing rapidly. In the past, many cleanup operations were handled by the Environmental Protection Agency. They have since been transferred to the Department of Homeland Security, which maintains much less strict environmental standards and tends to subcontract jobs to private companies. Subcontractors pay less and are subject to fewer regulations. They may also offer fewer benefits.

Let's Talk Trends

According to the Bureau of Labor Statistics, the number of hazardous materials and environmental cleanup workers will grow much faster than other professions through 2014. Because of increasing concerns over the environment, new legislation, and high turnover, many jobs for hazardous materials and environmental cleanup workers open up every year.

Your Typical Day

Here are the highlights of a typical day for an environmental cleanup worker.

✓ **Look for a problem.** Torrential rain has caused several rivers to overflow. The flooding could cause hazardous materials to wash into the environment. Your job is to find and fix potential problems.

✓ **Find a problem.** Patrolling the affected area in boats, you soon find a dangerous situation. A fuel oil tank is being buffeted by floodwaters. If it breaks open, it could kill fish, plants, and even people.

✓ **Fix the problem.** The problem isn't easily solved, since the tank is too big for your boat. Thinking quickly, you chain the tank to a nearby building and secure it. It can be removed later.

What Training You'll Need

Though the federal government requires licenses to work in hazardous materials cleanup, the actual level of training varies wildly. Some workers, such as those who transport hazardous materials, are required by law to have certain licenses and certifications. State workers are generally trained along those states' guidelines. Virginia, to cite one instance, requires 120 to 280 hours of training for members of its hazmat-response teams, and 24 hours of state-mandated training for officers. However, because much of the industry is being deregulated, it is difficult to make any definite claims. Training for workers in private industry varies widely. Some companies provide the standard 32- to 40-hour training programs for asbestos and lead abatement workers and for treatment, storage, and disposal workers. In other cases, workers have little or no training at all.

Standard training includes instruction in the nature of toxic materials, how to identify them, protective gear, health hazards, and decontamination. Many workers become certified to work with more than one hazardous material, since, if they discover one danger that they are not qualified to work with while removing another, they cannot continue the removal. Workers with multiple qualifications are in demand.

Workers who decommission nuclear facilities are the most extensively trained. In addition to the 40-hour asbestos, lead, and hazardous waste course, they must also learn how to deal with nuclear materials and radiation. This can take about three months.

Workers who have licenses are generally better paid. They are also required to take annual refresher courses to maintain their licenses.

The Inside Scoop: Q&A

Charles Crawford
Hazardous materials worker
New Orleans, Louisiana

Q: *How did you get your job?*

A: I started out transporting hazardous material on barges. My dad worked on a tugboat in oil distribution and I was encouraged to work in the business. I started out as a deckhand and I worked my way up and got my Merchant Mariners Document with a "person in charge-barge" with "dangerous liquids" and "LPG" endorsements, which is administered through the Coast Guard. It covers dangerous liquids and LPG (or Liquefied Petroleum Gas) cargos. Eventually, I became a shore tankerman. The difference is that on a boat, you work with the same barges and same cargos, while a shore tankerman goes wherever he's needed.

Q: *What do you like best about your job?*

A: The flexibility of taking days off. It's a pretty stressful job, especially working on the boat, so they're generous with the time off. On the boat, I'd work seven or eight months straight and then get four months off. After that, as a shore tankerman, well, I just liked working on land and being able to go home and sleep in my own bed!

Q: *What's the most challenging part of your job?*

A: You have to know everything about each product—its specific properties and dangers. Some chemicals simply can't be mixed; if you put one chemical into a tank with another chemical residue on it, you could get an undesired chemical reaction or, worse yet, an explosion. Also, you have to know a lot about barge structures and hull stresses for loading partial or split loads (multiple cargoes). And just because you're doing your job doesn't matter, since someone else might not be doing theirs on the other end of the pipeline. As a shore tankerman, you also have to take a first-responder scene commander class. If something goes wrong, whether due to human or mechanical error, you're in charge until

(Continued on next page)

(continued from previous page)

the proper scene commander arrives because, obviously, you're the most knowledgeable person on the accident that just happened. Your first priority is saving human life; your second is containing the problem, if possible—which usually goes a long way toward saving lives. Your immediate duties at an accident scene include analyzing the accident as the "first responder-scene commander" to determine the possible exposure hazard so you can coordinate the local authorities to what they need to do to evacuate the public to safety. Then you coordinate and participate in the cleanup teams. You remain the scene commander until relieved by the proper officials and then you participate in the investigation to determine the cause of the accident.

Q: *What are the keys to success as a hazardous materials cleanup worker?*

A: Don't think you know everything. If you think you know everything, then that's when you have an accident. If you walk away from a job without learning something, that's when you know you're doing something wrong. Just because you did it that way last week doesn't mean you'll do it that way this week.

What You Can Do Now

✴ Learn about the hazmat-cleanup industry. Try to make contacts where you would like to work.

✴ Pay attention in math and science classes. Find out what hazardous materials are and why they are dangerous. Learn to make mathematical calculations and conversions quickly.

✴ Take first aid courses and learn cardiopulmonary resuscitation (CPR). Being prepared for emergencies is good sense and a hiring plus.

How to Talk Like a Pro

Here are a few words you'll hear as a hazardous materials removal or environmental cleanup worker:

⭐ **OSHA** Pronounced OSH-ah, this is the Occupational Safety and Health Administration, in charge of preventing work-related illnesses and promoting safety. Many hazmat regulations come from OSHA.

⭐ **Hazard classes** A nine-part classification that shows exactly how a material is dangerous. Class 1, for instance, is explosives, while Class 7 is radioactive materials.

⭐ **First responder** "First responder" refers to the police, firefighters, paramedics, and other emergency services who are the first on the scene during a crisis.

How to Find a Job

One way to find work as a hazardous materials or environmental cleanup worker is to simply look in the newspaper. City and state agencies, as well as private companies, generally advertise in the classified sections. You may also send a résumé to the human resources departments of companies and these agencies. Also check both companies' and agencies' Web sites for openings, as well as the many sites that list job openings.

Another way to find work as a hazardous materials or environmental cleanup worker is word of mouth. If you know someone who works in this industry, ask them if they know of any opportunities.

Secrets for Success

See the suggestions below and turn to the appendix for advice on résumés and interviews.

⭐ Pay attention to detail. Both your safety and that of others lies on your actions.

⭐ Always listen to safety instructions. They're there for your benefit.

Reality Check

Cleaning up hazardous materials can be very dangerous and demanding. The quality of the workplace is also suffering from the weakening of standards and controls.

Some Other Jobs to Think About

✦ Construction worker. Asbestos and lead abatement workers share many skills with different construction workers, such as painters and paperhangers.

✦ Power-plant operator. Treatment, storage, and disposal workers, as well as decommissioning and decontamination workers, must be familiar with these systems.

✦ Police officer or firefighter. Like cleanup workers, police and firefighters keep people safe in the event of a disaster.

How You Can Move Up

✦ Gain certifications. Workers who are certified for more than one sort of material are in high demand.

✦ Become a supervisor. Though it takes additional training, supervisors make more than workers.

✦ Go into a related field. A decommissioning worker, for instance, may become a power-plant operator.

Web Sites to Surf

Laborers Learn. Education and resource site. Registration required. http://www.laborerslearn.org

Office of Hazardous Materials Safety. Learn about hazardous materials and cleanup. http://hazmat.dot.gov

Earn a good wage

Metalworker

Build skyscrapers, bridges, and other projects

Learn a skilled trade

Metalworker

Henry Bessemer's 1855 invention of an inexpensive method of making steel led to a revolution in building. New architectural marvels were made possible by Bessemer's new method. For instance, the Brooklyn Bridge, the world's first steel-wire suspension bridge, was built from 1870 to 1883. Steel-frame buildings could also be built much higher than old masonry structures. The first modern steel-frame skyscraper, the Home Insurance Building in Chicago, was built from 1884 to 1885. Other skyscrapers soon followed in cities such as New York and London, where land was valuable and it was cheaper to build up. None of this would have been possible, however, without skilled metalworkers to cut, bend, shape, and join the steel components. Today, metalworkers are still essential in the construction trades. According to the U.S. Department of Labor, there are about 106,000 ironworkers and 132,000 sheet metal workers in the U.S. construction industry.

Is This Job for You?

To find out if being a metalworker is right for you, read each of the following questions and answer "Yes" or "No."

Yes	No	**1.**	Do you work carefully, quickly, and precisely?
Yes	No	**2.**	Are you not afraid of heights?
Yes	No	**3.**	Do you like working with tools?
Yes	No	**4.**	Do you listen to directions?
Yes	No	**5.**	Do you like working outdoors?
Yes	No	**6.**	Are you in good physical shape?
Yes	No	**7.**	Can you lift heavy loads?
Yes	No	**8.**	Can you communicate in English and Spanish?
Yes	No	**9.**	Are you good at math and science?
Yes	No	**10.**	Do you not mind starting at the bottom?

If you answered "Yes" to most of these questions, perhaps you should consider a career as an metalworker. To find out more about this job, read on.

What You'll Do

There are several different types of metalworkers in the construction trades. *Structural and reinforcing iron and metalworkers* put iron and steel girders, columns, steel mesh, and other structural components in place on buildings, bridges, tunnels, highways, and other structures. They then secure them with welding, rivets, and other techniques. Such workers are often known by the old-fashioned title *ironworkers*, even though the material they work with is steel. Tools used in this trade are steel frames, cranes, derricks, connecting bars, welding torches, and other equipment. Ironworkers may also work restoring old buildings.

Reinforcing iron and rebar workers set rebar, or reinforcing bars, in the forms around which concrete is poured. The concrete's load-bearing ability and the rebar's flexibility add up to a material that is stronger than either alone. These workers may need to bend or cut the rebar, tie it together with wire, or weld it.

Sheet metal workers make, install, and maintain everything from duct systems to roofs, rain gutters, and rain spouts. Their job often overlaps with HVAC Technicians (Chapter 8). They must accurately cut and fabricate the components, install them neatly, and secure them.

Who You'll Work For

★ Commercial, residential, and industrial construction contractors—especially highway contractors and those that work on making new buildings
★ City, state, and the federal government

Where You'll Work

While sheet metal workers may fabricate some of the things they install in a shop, most metalworkers work outdoors in the heat of summer and cold of winter. Metalworkers can be found on any building or highway site, working for either private contractors or the government. Most metalworkers are not self-employed, since they need expensive materials, machines, and tools, as well as a large team, to perform their jobs.

Generally, metalworkers work a 40-hour week, though they may need to work overtime if a deadline is approaching. However, the work schedule itself can be very irregular. Metalworkers may find themselves out of work when a project ends. Bad weather can delay or cancel outdoor work. Because of this, the work tends to be seasonal. Metalworkers get more work in the summer and less in the winter. Those who live in places where the weather is generally good year-round, such as the South and Southwest, can work more days out of the year.

The work can be uncomfortable or even dangerous. Metalworkers deal with heavy, sometimes sharp, materials and possibly dangerous equipment such as welding torches. Some work takes place on the "high steel," constructing skyscrapers far above city streets. Metalworkers also need to lift heavy loads and sometimes bend, stretch, crouch, or otherwise work in uncomfortable positions.

Your Typical Day

Here are the highlights of a typical day for a metalworker working on the "high steel."

✓ **Unload the steel.** Today you'll be putting girders in place for an upper story of a skyscraper. The truck arrives in the morning with a load of steel beams. The first thing you have to do is unload and stack the beams.

✔ **Lift it up.** To lift, or *hoist*, the steel, you attach *slings,* or cables to it. You direct the hoist operator while a buddy holds the *tag line* that keeps the steel from swinging.

✔ **Place it and weld it.** The crane lifts the steel into place on the struc-ture. You then position and hold the steel in place with *connect-ing bars* and *spud wrenches.* You align the holes in the steel with holes in the structure, and, after using a laser level to make sure it is straight, you bolt the steel into place.

The Inside Scoop: Q&A

Remus Pop
Metalworker
New York, New York

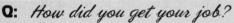

Q: *How did you get your job?*

A: I did a three-year trade school course in welding, structural reinforcing, and fabrication.

Q: *What do you like best about your job?*

A: The process of melting metal with electricity to produce one of the strongest bonds on earth! I also like the superstructures and the walk up in the sky.

Q: *What's the most challenging part of your job?*

A: Being a metalworker is one of the world's three most dangerous jobs. I'd have to say that so far as negative aspects go, it's a toss-up between the height, the weight of the steel and the equipment, the attention you have to pay to it, and the fact that you can easily die.

Q: *What are the keys to success as a metalworker?*

A: You need skill and courage.

What You Can Do Now

✷ Pay attention in math and shop classes. These will teach you skills you will need as an metalworker. Knowing Spanish, tech-nical drawing, and welding are also useful.

✴ Stay in good physical shape. Metalworking is demanding work.
✴ Research apprenticeship programs and trade schools in your area.

What Training You'll Need

While sheet metal workers sometimes learn on the job, in order to become a fully qualified metalworker and have the most job opportunities, it is best to begin as an apprentice. Apprenticeship programs last three to five years and include both on-the-job training and classroom instruction. They are overseen by the International Association of Bridge, Structural, Ornamental, and Reinforcing Iron Workers or local contractors association. In order to begin such a program, you will need to be 18 years old and in good health. Good hand-eye coordination, agility, balance, and space perception are essential. It is important not to be afraid of heights or subject to dizzy spells.

Apprentices begin with the simplest tasks, such as unloading materials and cleaning up. In the classroom, they learn math, how to read blueprints, basic architecture, welding, rigging, tool use and safety. As they progress, they are trusted with more difficult tasks, such as cutting beams and putting them in place. Sheet metal workers may also learn drafting, decorative metalworking, layout, and how to use computerized equipment.

On-the-job training often takes longer than formal apprenticeships and does not provide as complete training. Like apprentices, metalworkers who learn on the job begin with simple tasks and move up to more complex work.

How to Talk Like a Pro

Here are a few words you'll hear as an metalworker:

✴ **High steel** Working on a superstructure far above the ground, such as a skyscraper.
✴ **Tag line** A stabilizing rope used to keep steel from spinning when it's being lifted by a crane.
✴ **Spud wrench** A tool used to connect steel beams with connecting bars.

How to Find a Job

Apprenticeship programs can be difficult to get into. The best way is to inquire with local contractors and unions, which can guide you in the application process. Knowing someone who is already a metalworker can help, both by providing connections and getting letters of recommendation. Having completed a trade school program also helps.

For qualified metalworkers, work is usually found through the local union. Unions maintain job boards and also provide their members with other benefits, such as pensions and unemployment insurance. However, unions can be difficult to get into; you usually need to already know the trade and be working. Sometimes you can also find work with smaller contractors, state, local, and federal government jobs, and other employment in newspaper ads and online bulletin boards and job boards such as Craigslist (http://www.craisglist.org). Word of mouth is another way metalworkers find jobs—if a construction project is beginning and people you have worked with before are involved, they may recommend you to the employer. Always do a good job and give people a reason to recommend you!

Secrets for Success

See the suggestions below and turn to the appendix for advice on résumés and interviews.

- ✯ Pay attention to safety. Remember, other people are counting on you!
- ✯ Metalworkers are under three main stresses: To do good work and to do it quickly and safely. Be sure to balance all three.

Reality Check

Metalworking is hard and sometimes dangerous work. However, it also pays very well.

Some Other Jobs to Think About

- ✯ Construction laborer. Many metalworkers begin as construction laborers before beginning apprenticeship programs.
- ✯ Cement or brick mason. Masons are also skilled workers, but they don't have to work 300 feet in the air!

✴ Carpenter. Another skilled trade that isn't quite as strenuous as metalworking.

How You Can Move Up

✴ Become a construction supervisor. Metalworkers with experience can move up to become a foreman or supervisor. Knowledge of Spanish will help you communicate with your workers.

✴ Become an inspector. With their specialized knowledge of building construction, metalworkers are well situated to become state or city safety inspectors.

✴ Go into business for yourself. While most metalworkers are employed by large contractors, some, especially those working in decorative work, are self-employed.

Web Sites to Surf

International Association of Bridge, Structural, Ornamental, and Reinforcing Iron Workers. The ironworker's union; provides apprenticeship information. http://www.ironworkers.org

Associated Builders and Contractors, Workforce Development Department. More information on getting into the business. http://www.trytools.org

Work outdoors

Line-, Tower-, or Antenna-Crew Member

Work in a vital industry

Earn a very good wage

Line-, *Tower-*, *or Antenna-Crew Member*

The hurricane has wreaked havoc on the city. Thousands of homes and hundreds of businesses—including schools, hospitals, and nursing homes—are left without telephone lines or electrical power. Cell phone towers have been knocked down, and even high-speed Internet cables have been disabled. People's comfort, safety, and even their lives depend on these vital utilities. Thankfully, the line-, tower-, and antenna-crew members are on the job. As soon as it is safe to do so, they are out repairing the downed utility connections. Line-, tower-, and antenna-crew members are not only important to our economy—they are also very well paid. There are about 251,000 working in this vital job in the United States today.

Is This Job for You?

To find out if being an line-, tower-, or antenna-crew member is right for you, read each of the following questions and answer "Yes" or "No."

Yes	*No*	**1.**	Are you not afraid of heights?
Yes	*No*	**2.**	Are you physically fit?
Yes	*No*	**3.**	Do you like working outdoors?
Yes	*No*	**4.**	Are you good at math and science?
Yes	*No*	**5.**	Can you follow directions precisely?
Yes	*No*	**6.**	Can you lift heavy loads?
Yes	*No*	**7.**	Are you good with tools?
Yes	*No*	**8.**	Can you see in color?
Yes	*No*	**9.**	Do you have a good sense of balance?
Yes	*No*	**10.**	Are you careful?

If you answered "Yes" to most of these questions, you might consider a career as a line-, tower-, or antenna-crew member. To find out more, read on.

What You'll Do

No matter whether they work for an electric, telephone, wireless, or cable company, a line-, tower-, or antenna-crew member must know all about the system they work on. This means transformers, distribution systems, and substations for electrical crewmembers and fiber

Let's Talk Money

Line-, tower-, or antenna-crew members make better salaries than most non-college graduates. Their median income, according to 2006 figures from the U.S. Bureau of Labor Statistics, is $23.61 per hour, ranging from $13.31 to $32.54. Those who work for electric companies tend to make the most, and those who work for contractors, the least.

optic lines, routers, and telecommunications switches for those who work for telecommunications companies. Lines are installed by digging trenches or setting up utility poles and towers. You may need to use a *digger derrick*, which is a truck with an auger and crane, to set up a telephone pole, or a *trencher or cable plow* to cut a trench to lay wires. Then you string the cable along the poles, towers, or trench. You may need to climb the pole or go up in a *cherry picker*, (a truck-mounted bucket on a crane), to do this. The line is pulled up from a reel on a truck, insulators are attached, and the cable is pulled to the correct amount of tension before being attached. You may also need to attach devices to keep animals such as pigeons and squirrels from interfering with the line. You may also find yourself stringing cable between customers' homes or businesses and the utility poles.

Who You'll Work For

⭐ Utility companies
⭐ Telecommunications companies
⭐ Self-employment

Where You'll Work

Line-, tower-, or antenna-crew members often have to climb poles and towers and deal with dangerous high-voltage wires. They may also need to go into underground utility holes where toxic gasses can collect. Their work can thus be somewhat hazardous. It is therefore important that line-, tower-, or antenna-crew members use fall-prevention equipment, test for gas, pay careful attention to safety rules and regulations, and, above all, always use common sense. Line-, tower-, or antenna-crew members may also have to sit, stand, and kneel for long periods of time, as well as lift heavy

Let's Talk Trends

The number of line-, tower-, or antenna-crew members is expected to grow more slowly than the national average through 2014, according to the Bureau of Labor Statistics. Though many workers are retiring and the demand for electricity and other services is increasing, industry deregulation is pushing companies to cut costs as much as possible and do more with less workers.

equipment and drive and operate utility vehicles. For these reasons, it is important that line-, tower-, or antenna-crew members be in good physical shape.

Most line-, tower-, or antenna-crew members work forty-hour weeks. However, emergencies such as storms often require overtime to repair the damage. Most of the work, needless to say, is outdoors in the cold of winter, the heat of summer, and, very often, in bad weather conditions—though repairs are, of course, usually not started until a storm or other hazardous situation has stopped.

Your Typical Day

Here are the highlights of a typical day for a line-, tower-, or antenna-crew member installing a utility pole.

✓ **Dig a hole.** A recent hurricane has shown that the old wooden poles your company uses are inadequate, so you're installing new reinforced-concrete poles. The first thing you'll need to do in order to put up the pole is to make a foundation deep enough to take the weight. To do this you use a *digger derrick*, a truck that has an auger, or hole-digger, and a crane.

✓ **Put it up.** With the hole dug, you can use the digger derrick's crane to place the pole. Carefully and slowly, you lower it into place and erect it in a vertical position.

✓ **Rig it.** Now you need to go up and string the cable. Carefully climbing the pole, you attach insulators so that the non-conductive poles do not disrupt the flow of electricity. Your partner on the ground pulls the cables so that they have the right tension, and you attach them to the poles. Finally, you attach plastic shields so that squirrels can't get to the wires and short them out by chewing on them.

The Inside Scoop: Q&A

Anthony Riso
Line worker
Oakley, California

Q: *How did you get your job?*

A: I applied at my company as a utility worker hoping to get my foot in the door. At that time, I knew if I got the position, then I could start an apprenticeship and move on from there. It took me two-and-a-half years to finally get the job I wanted. I got the utility worker position, passed a series of mathematical tests, and started the three-year apprenticeship after passing the tests. I studied the basic electricity and solid state fundamentals books, got on-the-job training, and served my time in the trade learning the apprenticeship program. Basically, I was learning everything that applied to my job.

Q: *What do you like best about your job?*

A: Because I work for the local utility company, my job consists of replacing the power grid here in the Bay area. That consists of everything from changing out high-voltage transformers and breakers to scaling towers as tall as 300 feet to maintain power lines. The best part of my job is probably working in the air, not having a single worry, because at that moment of time, at that height, with that much danger and risk of death, my thought process and safety instincts are never clearer. You would be surprised how clear your head is at that time. It's an amazing rush.

Q: *What's the most challenging part of your job?*

A: The worst part is probably the down time. Every now and then, there's times where you run out of work for several days because of the heat. When it heats up and the demand for electricity is extremely high, you can't work or upgrade any equipment because you can't take them out of service. Supply and demand. Basic economics. I don't like standing around with nothing to do.

(Continued on next page)

(continued from previous page)

Q: *What are the keys to success as a line worker?*

A: One, you control what you want to achieve in life. You have the chance to do whatever you want. Two, always work hard for what you want. It will pay off in the long run, guaranteed. Three, always make smart and common-sense decisions. Life is a series of decisions and 99 percent of the time they are very easy decisions to make. The decisions are normally either yes or no, right or wrong, and good or bad. Just use common sense and make the right decision. That's the easiest decision to make.

What You Can Do Now

* Pay attention in school, especially in physics and mathematics classes.
* Stay in good physical shape. The line-, tower-, or antenna-crew member's job is a hard one!
* Research schools and training programs in your area.

What Training You'll Need

Most of a line-, tower-, or antenna-crew member's training is received on the job. This is often, but not always, through formal apprenticeships. These apprenticeships are often run by employers working in concert with unions such as the International Brotherhood of Electrical Workers, the Communications Workers of America, and the Utility Workers of America. They can last up to five years and combine practical, on-the-job training with classroom courses on such things as telecommunications systems, electronics, and physics. For apprentice electrical line workers, government regulations strictly set out the training and education that must be provided. You may start out as a ground worker, helper, or tree-trimmer clearing branches away from cables and power lines. As you progress, you will be given more responsible jobs, such as stringing cable and maintaining the system.

Companies who employ line-, tower-, or antenna-crew members often prefer if applicants have a working knowledge of electricity or electronics before hiring them. Courses that can help prepare you for this career are often offered through vocational or technical schools. Some schools, in cooperation with local employers and unions, offer certificate programs that emphasize hands-on work experience as a line-, tower-, or antenna-crew member. These training programs can help you get ahead. Another way to gain experience is in the armed forces. Many line-, tower-, and antenna-crew members first got their start this way.

If you want to apply to be a line-, tower-, or antenna-crew member, it is also helpful to know algebra and trigonometry. Being strong, unafraid of heights, and having good stamina and coordination are also necessary. Since cables are often color-coded, so is being able to see in color. Because you will need to operate company-owned vehicles, having a driver's license also helps.

How to Talk Like a Pro

Here are a few words you'll hear as an line-, tower-, or antenna-crew member:

- ☆ **Cherry picker** A bucket on a crane, used to reach utility wires.
- ☆ **Digger derrick** A truck with an auger for digging holes and a crane for putting up poles.
- ☆ **Conduit** A hollow pipe through which underground lines can be run.

How to Find a Job

The best way to find a job as a line-, tower-, or antenna-crew member is by asking local utility companies. It may be helpful to send your résumé to their human resources department and follow it up with a phone call. You can find their contact information in the phone book or on the Internet. Also keep your eyes open for opportunities in the Classifieds section of your local newspaper—where companies that hire line-, tower-, or antenna-crew members are likely to advertise—and on utility companies' Web sites.

Another way to look for an apprenticeship program is by contacting local large contractors and unions. It often helps to have a personal recommendation to get into these programs. If you choose to go to a trade or vocational school instead, many of these schools have job-placement programs that can help you find work after you graduate.

Some line-, tower-, or antenna-crew members are self-employed. Many of these are contractors who telecommunications companies pay to take care of customer service problems and installations.

Secrets for Success

See the suggestions below and turn to the appendix for advice on résumés and interviews.

★ Always be careful. It is when you get complacent that accidents happen.

★ Remember that people are counting on you. Be sure to do a good job the first time.

Reality Check

Line-, tower, and antenna-crew members are paid extremely well, but the job can be hard, stressful, and dangerous.

Some Other Jobs to Think About

★ Electrician. Electricians also work with electricity, but don't have to climb utility poles.

★ Phone/cable installer. Work inside people's homes instead of outdoors.

★ Radio and telecommunications installers and repairers. Install and repair radio and telecommunications equipment.

How You Can Move Up

★ Stay on the job. With seniority comes more responsibility—and more money.

★ Become a supervisor or trainer. Employees in these positions oversee other workers.

★ Go back to school. Higher supervisory positions often require more education.

Web Sites to Surf

Utility Workers Union of America. The union for many line-, tower-, and antenna-crew members. http://www.uwua.net

International Brotherhood of Electrical Workers. Another union that many electrical workers belong to. Includes apprenticeship guidelines. http://ibew.org

Make a good wage

Road-Crew Member

Build roads, bridges, and highways

Enjoy good job security

Road-Crew Member

Among the wonders of the ancient world was the highway system of Rome. The Romans built miles of straight, well-drained, stone-topped roads. These roads helped people and goods move quickly from one place to another. Because of this, the Roman economy grew and the Roman Empire was able to conquer and control a vast amount of territory. Today roads and highways are no less important to government and commerce. They allow goods and people to travel and emergency vehicles to reach people in need. The people who build and maintain these roads and highways are road-crew members. According to the U.S. Department of Labor, there are 348,000 people working in highway and road construction and 143,000 in maintenance in the United States.

Is This Job for You?

To find out if being a road-crew member is right for you, read each of the following questions and answer "Yes" or "No."

Yes	No	**1.**	Are you in good physical shape?
Yes	No	**2.**	Do you not mind working nights and weekends?
Yes	No	**3.**	Do you work well as part of a team?
Yes	No	**4.**	Can you follow directions?
Yes	No	**5.**	Can you lift heavy loads?
Yes	No	**6.**	Do you not mind getting your hands dirty?
Yes	No	**7.**	Are you careful?
Yes	No	**8.**	Do you like working outdoors?
Yes	No	**9.**	Can you operate heavy equipment?
Yes	No	**10.**	Can you speak Spanish?

If you answered "Yes" to most of these questions, you might want to consider a career as a road-crew member. To find out more about this job, read on.

What You'll Do

Road-crew members make and maintain roads and highways. After civil engineers select a site and the surveyors mark out how it will be laid, the land needs to be cleared and leveled. Trees and rocks must be removed. If the road is to be in a mountainous area, sometimes sheer rock must be blasted. Sometimes drainage ditches, storm drains, or wildlife underpasses must be put in. Then the road must be built up layer by layer—first crushed rock, then concrete, and then asphalt. Each layer must be smoothed and graded, so that it is higher in the middle and water will run off rather than collecting in pools. Finally, traffic lanes and directions are painted on the new asphalt.

If an existing road is being expanded, then road-crew members must move existing traffic aside by placing *flagmen* (workers who direct traffic), signs, traffic cones, and concrete barriers. They may need to demolish an existing road with jackhammers and other tools. Road-crew members may also work on bridges and tunnels.

Maintenance includes many tasks that keep our transportation system usable. Road-crew members who maintain bridges, roads, and highways patch broken and eroded concrete and damaged guardrails. They place highway markers and signs, as well as snow fences, and may mow and remove brush.

Who You'll Work For

★ City, state, and the federal government

Let's Talk Trends

Though the number of construction laborers in general will grow more slowly than average through 2014, road-crew members' services will be needed to repair existing highways and roads. Employment of road-crew members should therefore remain somewhat stable, and high turnover means that new workers will need to be hired. According to the Bureau of Labor Statistics, this means that road-crew members can expect much faster than average growth.

✴ Private contractors hired by governments to work on roads and highways

✴ Large construction companies who contract for road repair

Where You'll Work

Road-crew members of course work outside. This means that the work is seasonal. Bad weather can delay construction and result in the loss of a day's wages. As with all construction trades, road-crew members tend to get more work in the summer and less in the winter. However, those who live in places where the weather is generally good year-round, such as the South and Southwest, can work more days out of the year. On the other hand, harsh northern winters damage roads and make more work for repair crews to do. Generally speaking, road-crew members work 40-hour weeks, though a rush project may result in overtime and overtime pay.

Road-crew members use specialized equipment such as jackhammers, earth tampers, asphalt-paving machines, graders, and steamrollers. Though this construction equipment can be noisy and uncomfortable to use, power tools can be dangerous or lead to repetitive-stress injuries, workers who deal with such things are well paid. The work also can be very strenuous. You may be working with hot asphalt on a 100-degree summer day or lifting heavy loads. This isn't a job for people who mind getting dirty and sweaty—but if you like working outdoors, even in heat, cold, and rain, you'll enjoy being a road-crew member.

Your Typical Day

Here are the highlights of a typical day for a road-crew member.

✔ **Rip it up.** Today you'll be resurfacing a section of highway. First, though, you'll have to rip up the old asphalt with a jackhammer.

✔ **Make the grade.** Before putting the new surface on, the highway has to be leveled, or graded. Highways are actually built a bit higher in the middle, so rainwater runs off.

✔ **Smooth it out.** Now that the road is graded, the asphalt truck spreads hot asphalt, and it's smoothed out by a steamroller.

The Inside Scoop: Q&A

Epillio Mejia
Road-crew member
New York, New York

Q: *How did you get your job?*

A: One of my friends knew the boss. He brought me to the job, and I liked it. I've been working here fifteen years.

Q: *What do you like best about your job?*

A: I like working outside and I like that it's always a different place and a different job—not in an office.

Q: *What's the most challenging part of your job?*

A: Well, it's hot in the summer and cold in the winter. Also, every job site is different, which means you've got to do different things—it presents different challenges.

Q: *What are the keys to success as a road-crew member?*

A: Work hard. If you find something you like to do, work hard. And always put everything into it. You gotta use your *fuerza*—your strength.

What You Can Do Now

- Pay attention in school, especially in mathematics, Spanish, and shop classes.
- Stay fit. The better shape you're in, the more you'll like working as a road-crew member.
- Learn to drive. Often you will need to drive yourself to and from work sites.

What Training You'll Need

Most road-crew members receive informal on-the-job training. Road-crew members often start with the most basic tasks, such as unloading materials, waving cars away, and putting out traffic cones. As time goes on, they are given more responsible tasks, such as grading roads and spreading asphalt. Some members of the team may have specific jobs, such as placing barriers, clearing brush, or operating jackhammers.

Operating machines such as bulldozers and steamrollers may require doing an apprenticeship or attending a trade school. In general, the more complicated the work, the more likely you will need formal training. Some employers offer apprenticeship programs through the International Union of Operating Engineers or the Associated General Contractors of America. Such programs include 3 years, or 6,000 hours, of on-the-job training, with 144 hours of classroom instruction per year. For more on learning to operate construction machinery, see Chapter 2, on construction laborers and construction equipment operators.

How to Talk Like a Pro

Here are a few words you'll hear as a road-crew member:

- ✯ **Flagman** A worker with a flag who directs traffic away from where a road crew is working.
- ✯ **Grader** A machine that levels, or grades, a roadway so that it is at a constant slope.
- ✯ **Asphalt heater** A machine that keeps the asphalt hot, so that it can be spread on the road.

How to Find a Job

Most road-crew members work for local or state governments either directly or through another company that signs a contract to work on local roads. They can be hired in many ways. State governments are usually required to publicly announce open job positions. You should therefore look on contractors' and state governments' Web sites and in newspaper help-wanted ads. Look up local contractors and construction companies in the phone book or on the Internet. Some will even take walk-ins, though it is helpful to have a personal reference at the company.

Another way of finding work in construction is a local joint labor-management apprenticeship committee, an apprenticeship agency, and state employment services. These are run by unions and also by trade organizations, contractors, and government agencies to oversee apprenticeships, and can often be found online. If you already have some experience in construction, unions often operate job-placement services for their members. However, unions often require you to already be working before joining. Word of mouth is also important, if you know who or where to ask.

Secrets for Success

See the suggestions below and turn to the appendix for advice on résumés and interviews.

✴ Learn a trade, such as operating construction vehicles. Skilled workers are both more in demand and better paid than unskilled ones.

✴ Work well with your coworkers. Being on a road crew is all about teamwork.

Reality Check

Being on a road crew is hard, tiring work. There is often little upward mobility. However, it can pay very well and provide a good income while you receive other training.

Some Other Jobs to Think About

✴ Construction equipment operator. Skilled equipment operators are paid more than ordinary workers.

✴ Construction laborer. Work on buildings in urban areas rather than on roads.

✴ Tower-, line-, or antenna-crew member. These workers also work outdoors, have a lot of responsibility, and are very well paid.

How You Can Move Up

✴ Learn a skill. Road-crew work tends to be less skilled. Use your time as a road-crew member to go to trade school and learn a trade. Skilled workers tend to be paid more.

✴ Become a supervisor. With enough seniority, you can advance to a supervisory position. Because today many road-crew members' first language is Spanish, it helps to be able to communicate both in English and Spanish.

✮ Find a different job. State agencies often hire from within. While working on a road crew, keep your eyes open for other jobs with the state (or city) Department of Highways, such as truck driving.

Web Sites to Surf

Laborers Learn. An education and training resource for Construction Laborers. Registration required.   http://www.laborerslearn.org

International Union of Operating Engineers. The IUOE is the union for construction-equipment operators.   http://www.iuoe.org

Appendix A

Unlock your network

Get your résumé ready

Ace your interview

Putting Your Best Foot Forward

When 20-year-old Justin Schulman started job-hunting for a position as a fitness trainer—the first step toward managing a fitness facility—he didn't mess around. "I immediately opened the Yellow Pages and started calling every number listed under health and fitness, inquiring about available positions," he recalls. Schulman's energy and enterprise paid off: He wound up with interviews that led to several offers of part-time work.

Schulman's experience highlights an essential lesson for job seekers: There are plenty of opportunities out there, but jobs won't come to you—especially the career-oriented, well-paying ones that that you'll want to stick with over time. You've got to seek them out.

Uncover Your Interests

Whether you're in high school or bringing home a full-time paycheck, the first step toward landing your ideal job is assessing your interests. You need to figure out what makes you tick. After all, there is a far greater chance that you'll enjoy and succeed in a career that taps into your passions, inclinations, and natural abilities. That's what happened with career-changer Scott Rolfe. He was already 26 when he realized he no longer wanted to work in the food industry. "I'm an avid outdoorsman," Rolfe says, "and I have an appreciation for natural resources that many people take for granted." Rolfe turned his passions into his ideal job as a forestry technician.

If you have a general idea of what your interests are, you're far ahead of the game. You may know that you're cut out for a health care career, for instance, or one in business. You can use a specific volume of Great Careers with a High School Diploma to discover what position to target. If you are unsure of your direction, check out the whole range of volumes to see the scope of jobs available.

You can also use interest inventories and skills-assessment programs to further pinpoint your ideal career. Your school or public librarian or guidance counselor should be able to help you locate such assessments. Web sites, such as America's Career InfoNet (http ://www.acinet.org) and Jobweb.com, also offer interest inventories.

You'll find suggestions for Web sites related to specific careers at the end of each chapter in any Great Careers with a High School Diploma volume.

Unlock Your Network

The next stop toward landing the perfect job is networking. The word may make you cringe, but networking is simply introducing yourself and exchanging job-related and other information that may prove helpful to one or both of you. That's what Susan Tinker-Muller did. Quite a few years ago, she struck up a conversation with a fellow passenger on her commuter train. Little did she know that the natural interest she expressed in the woman's accounts payable department would lead to news about a job opening there. Tinker-Muller's networking landed her an entry-level position in accounts payable with MTV Networks. She is now the accounts payable administrator.

Tinker-Muller's experience illustrates why networking is so important. Fully 80 percent of openings are *never* advertised, and more than half of all employees land their jobs through networking, according to the U.S. Bureau of Labor Statistics. That's 8 out of 10 jobs that you'll miss if you don't get out there and talk with people. And don't think you can bypass face-to-face conversations by posting your résumé on job sites like Craigslist, Monster.com, and Hotjobs.com and then waiting for employers to contact you. That's so mid-1990s! Back then, tens of thousands, if not millions, of job seekers diligently posted their résumés on scores of sites. Then they sat back and waited . . . and waited . . . and waited. You get the idea. Big job sites have their place, of course, but relying solely on an Internet job search is about as effective throwing your résumé into a black hole.

Begin your networking efforts by making a list of people to talk to: teachers, classmates (and their parents), anyone you've worked with, neighbors, members of your church, synogogue, temple or mosque, and anyone you've interned or volunteered with. You can also expand your networking opportunities through the student sections of industry associations; attending or volunteering at industry events, association conferences, career fairs; and through job-shadowing. Keep in mind that only rarely will any of the people on your list be in a position to offer you a job. But whether they know it or not, they probably know someone who knows someone who is. That's why your networking goal is not to ask for a job but the name of someone to talk with. Even when you network with an employer, it's wise to say something like, "You may not have any positions available, but would you know someone I could talk with to find out more about what it's like to work in this field?"

Also, keep in mind that networking is a two-way street. For instance, you may be talking with someone who has a job opening that isn't appropriate for you. If you can refer someone else to the employer, either person may well be disposed to help you someday in the future.

Dial-Up Help

Call your contacts directly, rather than e-mail them. (E-mails are too easy for busy people to ignore, even if they don't mean to.) Explain that you're a recent graduate; that Mr. Jones referred you; and that you're wondering if you could stop by for 10 or 15 minutes at your contact's convenience to find out a little more about how the industry works. If you leave this message as a voicemail, note that you'll call back in a few days to follow up. If you reach your contact directly, expect that they'll say they're too busy at the moment to see you. Ask, "Would you mind if I check back in a couple of weeks?" Then jot down a note in your date book or set up a reminder in your computer calendar and call back when it's time. (Repeat this above scenario as needed, until you get a meeting.)

Once you have arranged to talk with someone in person, prep yourself. Scour industry publications for insightful articles; having up-to-date knowledge about industry trends shows your networking contacts that you're dedicated and focused. Then pull together questions about specific employers and suggestions that will set you apart from the job-hunting pack in your field. The more specific your questions (for instance, about one type of certification versus another), the more likely your contact will see you as an "insider," worthy of passing along to a potential employer. At the end of any networking meeting, ask for the name of someone else who might be able to help you further target your search.

Get a Lift

When you meet with a contact in person (as well as when you run into someone fleetingly), you need an "elevator speech." This is a summary of up to two minutes that introduces who you are, as well as your experience and goals. An elevator speech should be short enough to be delivered during an elevator ride with a potential employer from the ground level to a high floor. In it, it's helpful to show that 1) you know the business involved; 2) you know the company; 3) you're qualified (give your work and educational information); and 4) you're goal-oriented, dependable, and hardworking. You'll be surprised how much information you can include in two minutes. Practice this speech in front of a mirror until you have the key points down very well. It should sound natural though, and you should come across as friendly, confident, and assertive. Remember, good eye contact needs to be part of your presentation as well as your everyday approach when meeting prospective employers or leads.

Get Your Résumé Ready

In addition to your elevator speech, another essential job-hunting tool is your résumé. Basically, a résumé is a little snapshot of you in words, reduced to one 8½ x 11-inch sheet of paper (or, at most, two sheets). You need a résumé whether you're in high school, college, or the workforce, and whether you've never held a job or have had many.

At the top of your résumé should be your heading. This is your name, address, phone numbers, and your e-mail address, which can be a sticking point. E-mail addresses such as sillygirl@yahoo.com or drinkingbuddy@hotmail.com won't score you any points. In fact they're a turn-off. So if you dreamed up your address after a night on the town, maybe it's time to upgrade. (And while we're on the subject, these days, potential employers often check Myspace pages, personal blogs, and Web sites. What's posted there has been known to cost candidates job offers.)

The first section of your résumé is a concise Job Objective: "Entry-level agribusiness sales representative seeking a position with a leading dairy cooperative." These days, with word-processing software, it's easy and smart to adapt your job objective to the position for which you're applying. An alternative way to start a résumé, which some recruiters prefer, is to rework the Job Objective into a Professional Summary. A Professional Summary doesn't mention the position you're seeking, but instead focuses on your job strengths: e.g., "Entry-level agribusiness sales rep; strengths include background in feed, fertilizer, and related markets and ability to contribute as a member of a sales team." Which is better? It's your call.

The body of a résumé typically starts with your Job Experience. This is a chronological list of the positions you've held (particularly the ones that will help you land the job you want). Remember: Never, never fudge anything. It is okay, however, to include volunteer positions and internships on the chronological list, as long as they're noted for what they are.

Next comes your Education section. Note: It's acceptable to flip the order of your Education and Job Experience sections if you're still in high school or don't have significant work experience. Summarize any courses you've taken in the job area you're targeting, any certifications you've achieved, relevant computer knowledge, special seminars, or other school-related experience that will distinguish you. Include your grade average if it's more than 3.0. Don't worry if you haven't finished your degree. Simply write that you're currently enrolled in your program (if you are).

In addition to these elements, other sections may include professional organizations you belong to and any work-related achievements, awards, or recognition you've received. Also, you can have a section for your interests, such as playing piano or soccer (and include any notable achievements regarding your interests, for instance, placed third in Midwest Regional Piano Competition). You should also note other special abilities, such as "Fluent in French," or "Designed own Web site." These sorts of activities will reflect well on you whether or not they are job-related.

You can either include your references or simply note, "References Upon Request." Be sure to ask your references permission to use their name, and alert them to the fact that they may be contacted, before you include them on your résumé. For more information on résumé writing, check out Web sites such as http://www.resume.monster.com.

Craft Your Cover Letter

When you apply for a job either online or by mail, it's appropriate to include a cover letter. A cover letter lets you convey extra information about yourself than doesn't fit or isn't always appropriate in your résumé. For instance, in a cover letter, you can and should mention the name of anyone who referred you to the job. You can go into some detail about the reason you're a great match, given the job description. You can also address any questions that might be raised in the potential employer's mind (for instance, a gap in your résumé). Don't, however, ramble on. Your cover letter should stay focused on your goal: to offer a strong, positive impression of yourself and persuade the hiring manager that you're worth an interview. Your cover letter gives you a chance to stand out from the other applicants and sell yourself. In fact, 23 percent of hiring managers say a candidate's ability to relate his or her experience to the job at hand is a top hiring consideration, according to a Careerbuilder.com survey.

You can write a positive, yet concise cover letter in three paragraphs: An introduction containing the specifics of the job you're applying for; a summary of why you're a good fit for the position and what you can do for the company; and a closing with a request for an interview, your contact information, and thanks. Remember to vary the structure and tone of your cover letter. For instance, don't begin every sentence with "I."

Ace Your Interview

Preparation is the key to acing any job interview. This starts with researching the company or organization you're interviewing with. Start with the firm, group, or agency's own Web site. Explore it thoroughly, read about their products and services, their history, and sales and marketing information. Check out their news releases, links that they provide, and read up on, or Google, members of the management team to get an idea of what they may be looking for in their employees.

Sites such as http://www.hoovers.com enable you to research companies across many industries. Trade publications in any industry (such as *Food Industry News*, *Hotel Business*, and *Hospitality Technology*) are also available at online or in hard copy at many college or public libraries. Don't forget to make a phone call to contacts you have in the organization to get a better idea of the company culture.

Preparation goes beyond research, however. It includes practicing answers to common interview questions:

✯ *Tell me about yourself.* Don't talk about your favorite bands or your personal history; give a brief summary of your background and interest in the particular job area.

✯ *Why do you want to work here?* Here's where your research into the company comes into play; talk about the firm's strengths and products or services.

✴ *Why should we hire you?* Now is your chance to sell yourself as a dependable, trustworthy, effective employee.

✴ *Why did you leave your last job?* Keep your answer short; never bad-mouth a previous employer. You can always say something simple, such as, "It wasn't a good fit, and I was ready for other opportunities."

Rehearse your answers, but don't try to memorize them. Responses that are natural and spontaneous come across better. Trying to memorize exactly what you want to say is likely to both trip you up and make you sound robotic.

As for the actual interview, to break the ice, offer a few pleasant remarks about the day, a photo in the interviewer's office, or something else similar. Then, once the interview gets going, listen closely and answer the questions you're asked, versus making any other point that you want to convey. If you're unsure whether your answer was adequate, simply ask, "Did that answer the question?" Show respect, good energy, and enthusiasm, and be upbeat. Employers are looking for workers who are enjoyable to be around, as well as good workers. Show that you have a positive attitude and can get along well with others by not bragging during the interview, overstating your experience, or giving the appearance of being too self-absorbed. Avoid one-word answers, but at the same time don't blather. If you're faced with a silence after giving your response, pause for a few seconds, and then ask, "Is there anything else you'd like me to add?" Never look at your watch and turn your cell phone off before an interview.

Near the interview's end, the interviewer is likely to ask you if you have any questions. Make sure that you have a few prepared, for instance:

✴ *"Tell me about the production process."*
✴ *"What's your biggest short-term challenge?"*
✴ *"How have recent business trends affected the company?"*
✴ *"Is there anything else that I can provide you with to help you make your decision?"*
✴ *"When will you make your hiring decision?"*

During a first interview, never ask questions like, "What's the pay?" "What are the benefits?" or "How much vacation time will I get?"

Find the Right Look

Appropriate dress and grooming is also essential to interviewing success. For business jobs and many other occupations, it's appropriate to come to an interview in a nice (not stuffy) suit. However, different fields have various dress codes. In the music business, for instance, "business casual" reigns for many jobs. This is a slightly modified look, where slacks and a jacket are just fine for a man, and a nice skirt and blouse and jacket or sweater are acceptable for a woman. Dressing overly "cool" will usually backfire.

In general, tend to all the basics from shoes (no sneakers, sandals, or overly high heels) to outfits (no short skirts for women). Women should also avoid attention-getting necklines. Keep jewelry to a minimum. Tattoos and body jewelry are becoming more acceptable, but if you can take out piercings (other than a simple stud in your ear), you're better off. Similarly, unusual hairstyles or colors may bias an employer against you, rightly or wrongly. Make sure your hair is neat and acceptable (consider getting a haircut). Also go light on the makeup, self-tanning products, body scents, and other grooming agents. Don't wear a baseball cap or any other type of hat, and by all means, take off your sunglasses!

Beyond your physical appearance, you already know to be well bathed to minimize odor (leave your home early if you tend to sweat, so you can cool off in private), use a breath mint (especially if you smoke) make good eye contact, smile, speak clearly using proper English (or Spanish), use good posture (don't slouch), offer a firm handshake, and arrive within five minutes of your interview. (If you're unsure of where you're going, Mapquest or Google Map it and consider making a dry run to the site so you won't be late.) First impressions can make or break your interview.

Remember to Follow Up

After your interview, send a thank-you note. This thoughtful gesture will separate you from most of the other candidates. It demonstrates your ability to follow through, and it catches your prospective employer's attention one more time. In a 2005 Careerbuilder.com survey, nearly 15 percent of 650 hiring managers said they wouldn't hire someone who failed to send a thank-you letter after the interview. Thirty-two percent say they would still consider the candidate, but would think less of him or her.

So do you hand write or e-mail the thank you letter? The fact is that format preferences vary. One in four hiring managers prefer to receive a thank-you note in e-mail form only; 19 percent want the e-mail, followed up with a hard copy; 21 percent want a typed hard-copy only, and 23 percent prefer just a handwritten note. (Try to check with an assistant on the format your potential employer prefers). Otherwise, sending an e-mail and a handwritten copy is a safe way to proceed.

Winning an Offer

There are no sweeter words to a job hunter than, "We'd like to hire you." So naturally, when you hear them, you may be tempted to jump at the offer. *Don't.* Once an employer wants you, he or she will usually give you some time to make your decision and get any questions you may have answered. Now is the time to get specific about salary, benefits, and negotiate some of these points. If you haven't already done so, check out salary ranges for your position and area of the country on sites such as Payscale.com, Salary.com, and Salaryexpert.com (basic info is free; specific requests are not). Also find out what sort of benefits similar jobs offer. Then don't be afraid to negotiate in a diplomatic way. Asking for better terms is reasonable and expected. You may worry that asking the employer to bump up his or her offer may jeopardize your job, but handled intelligently, negotiating for yourself may in fact be a way to impress your future employer and get a better deal for yourself.

After you've done all the hard work that successful job-hunting requires, you may be tempted to put your initiative into autodrive. However, the efforts you made to land your job—from clear communication to enthusiasm—are necessary now to pave your way to continued success. As Danielle Little, a human-resources assistant, says, "You must be enthusiastic and take the initiative. There is an urgency to prove yourself and show that you are capable of performing any and all related tasks. If your manager notices that you have potential, you will be given additional responsibilities, which will help advance your career." So do your best work on the job, and build your credibility. Your payoff will be career advancement and increased earnings.